Jessica's Journey

Triumph Through Tragedy

M.J. MICHAELS

This Book is based on the true story of Jessica's life and death and all that God did in the midst of the suffering of His children. However, some of the names and minor details have been changed to protect the privacy of involved.

This book is dedicated to those who have gone before us. May they rest in peace in the strong and loving arms of Jesus.

Jessica's Journey

Triumph Through Tragedy

Prologue

I DIDN'T START OUT to write this story. It was thrust upon me by Almighty God. I was just innocently driving to work one morning and out of the blue, I suddenly sensed a bright light coming down from the heavens and surrounding my car. I knew those around me wouldn't be able to see my car bathed in a golden light, and I couldn't really "see" it either, except in my mind's eye. I sensed it was there. The stoplight before me turned red, which was good because it was then I heard the voice of God firmly and loudly speak His command in my spirit. I looked around just to make sure no one else heard thunder, because that is what His voice sounded like - thunder. Now I understand the phrase, "His thunderous voice."

"You will write Jessica's story," the Great I Am said. I was so taken aback, I couldn't speak. Jessica was a sister of my dear friend, Joy. She had been brutally murdered five years earlier, and frankly I hadn't thought of Jessica in a long time.

"You will write her story," I heard again. I suddenly saw myself in a great hall. I was an emaciated figure with no hair. My clothes were rags and I was kneeling prostrate before the great white throne. It was so high and mighty, that I could only see the hem of the royal robes and the base of the throne. The robes looked like great swirling waves but there was no movement. I was a speck before the Holy One. The One who EVERY knee WILL bow before someday. There will be no choice. I began to sob in thankfulness that I was allowed to be there in His presence.

This all transpired in a matter of moments and as the stoplight turned to green, I continued to drive. In the midst of my sobs, an intense burning grew in my chest. Mixed within the sensation was incredible excitement. It was a strange event—to know where I was and be able to operate my car, yet to "be" somewhere else in spirit. I have never before nor since had such a profound encounter.

The day passed slowly but that night, I began writing. Feeling obsessed with the call of God, I typed for two hours. Words poured out of me so quickly, I had trouble keeping up with the flow. Adrenaline was pumping through my veins as my thoughts raced. I spent the night typing and praying for God to show me the way. I hadn't talked to my friend, Joy, about her sister in a long time. Would she think I was crazy? How would her parents react?

But the thoughts wouldn't go away, so every time I had a few minutes to myself, I typed.

I knew this was not to be my story. It was God's. I made a date to talk with Joy and tell her about my experience. Meanwhile, I prayed God would open her heart to understand. I mean, really, how do you go to someone and tell them you are writing about their personal information? *Their* loss. Time passed as I waited to meet with my friend and I began to realize that if God had really spoken to me, then He was certainly capable of speaking to Joy.

The day came and I sat down to tell Joy what I had experienced. As I spoke, she immediately began to cry. "God is amazing," she said over and over. "You don't know the backstory on this, do you?" she asked.

"I didn't know there was a backstory," I replied.

"My dad has been trying to get this story written for five years. He has hired a series of people and none of them have done the job. There have been constant roadblocks and it breaks my heart to see my dad struggle with this. Just yesterday I was asking the Lord to show me what to do and to bring the right person to get this done so my dad's heart can settle." We hugged and cried and laughed out loud about how the Lord was working behind the scenes to bring this book to fruition.

So here it is. After months of meetings with the

family, meetings with the Lord, and typing long into the night, I humbly give you the story of God's incredible work through the death of one of His children. May He receive all the glory for this because after all, it is HIS story.

Chapter 1
The Finding

"STEVE, SHE IS NOT answering her phone." I heard the panic in my wife's voice. She was due at her doctor's appointment in less than an hour, and didn't want to be late.

"Maury, she might be in the shower or on her way and can't hear her phone." I was trying to be optimistic and calm my wife's fears, but while my words were positive, my feelings were anything but.

How can she do that to her mom? She knows how anxious Maury gets before her appointments. Jessica better have a good reason for upsetting her.

"Maury, if she doesn't show up in the next ten minutes, call me back, and I will leave work and come pick you up."

"All right," she said quietly. I hung up with a sigh. Of all the days for Jessica to bail. I'd just expanded my business and couldn't leave the men right now. After all, my new project manager started two days ago and was still learning the ropes.

Jessica had always been attentive to her mom's needs but sometimes she can get so distracted with life she doesn't follow through. "I better not find out she is asleep," I mumbled under my breath.

Maury had endured a complicated surgery, six weeks earlier and couldn't drive yet, so Jessica had promised to take her mom to the doctor for today's appointment.

I was sitting in my office, going over crew lists and thinking about where to send them to maximize their time, when my phone rang.

Pulling my phone out of my pocket, I saw my wife's name light up. Ugh. There it is, I thought. She hasn't followed through with her promise, and now I'm the one who has to leave MY job to do HER job. I am so mad I could punch the wall.

It was December 15th, for Pete's sake, and one of our busiest times of the year. Not only were contractors trying to wrap up projects for the holidays, our family always put on charity functions for sick children. Maury loved giving and I did too, and still do, but there is always a lot of pressure this time of year with work, family, and reaching out to the less fortunate. There are lots of demands on my time and little time for those demands. I definitely did *not* need Jessica to bail on her promises during such a stressful time.

"Mike," I called out the door. "I've got to go out for about an hour. Do you think you're ready to fly solo for a while?" "Sure thing, boss. Not to worry. If I get stuck, I'll give you a call."

"Thanks, Mike. I'll be in around noon."

Mike was a nice kid, thirty-three years old, married with two little kids, and a hard worker. He grew up around construction, so he understood the importance of getting the right crews to our customers. One mess up on the schedule and it slowed down every project. Having the wrong supplies at the wrong job can hurt our reputation in the community, and I was building my name as a contractor who cared enough to do it right the first time. I was not willing to let that slip through my hands. If I had to take Maury to the doctor, I was glad I had Mike to rely on.

My phone was still ringing as I walked out the door and toward my car. Maybe Jessica has finally shown up, I thought. She was probably running late and as always, Maury jumped the gun on worrying. She does that well.

"Hey, Maury, is she there?" I asked into the phone as I turned and headed back toward the store.

"No. Steve, something is wrong. I feel it. I am so worried. Please find Jessica." Maury's voice was rising in panic and I rolled my eyes as I walked. She had always been a worrier, especially where the children were concerned. Maury didn't let the girls spend the night at their friends' houses until they were twelve years old. That decision had been "for their safety" and I hadn't had the chance to vote on the subject.

Maury is a petite, soft-spoken woman who looks somewhat fragile, but where her children were concerned, she is a "mother bear" who would take anyone down if she sensed danger of any kind. One time she took on the whole PTA when it was decided the students would be allowed to go on overnight sporting events without chaperones. It was an uphill battle, but by the time Maury was done, not only did the trips require a certain number of adults on each bus, she had a long list of parent volunteers signed up for the year. She can be a powerhouse when necessary, and that is one of the things I have always loved about her.

"What do you want me to do, Maury?" I asked. "Take you to the doctor or go find your daughter? Which one? I can't do both at the same time," I practically shouted into the phone. I had been at work early after being up late and wasn't at all in the mood for fulfilling Jessica's promise to her mother and then taking more work time to track down my wayward daughter. *Why today of all days, Jessica?* Maury went silent.

"Okay, okay. I'll be right there to pick you up and then I'll go see what's up with Jessica," I said, resigned. I needed to calm down and not let this get under my skin. My blood pressure was high enough as it was, and I needed to control my reactions toward Maury. She wasn't a well woman and didn't need the extra stress. I lowered my voice and almost whispered into the phone, "I love you, Maury. Don't worry. I'll take care of everything. You just get your shoes on and I'll be home soon." I hung up and turned back toward the car.

Opening the door and climbing in, I sat quietly for a moment, letting the warmth of the car calm me and hopefully, sweat out some of the toxic feelings I was experiencing. I bowed my forehead to the steering wheel. "God, I am so tired of this," I whispered. "Was I stupid to expand the business at my age? I mean, with Maury so sick. She needs me more now, and I'm so torn with work's demands and trying to be with her to meet her needs. God, please show me the way. Calm my spirit so I can be a calming influence on my wife. And help me to not kill Jessica when I find her." I lifted my head, turned the ignition, put the car in drive and drove out of the parking lot toward home.

Ten minutes later, I turned the corner and saw Maury standing at the end of our driveway…waiting. *Good grief, Maury. Can you give me time to drive home? She can be the most impatient woman.*

I drove up beside her and started to roll my window down but it was useless. She was already around the car and pulling the door open to get in. She didn't speak, just fastened her seat belt and looked straight ahead.

"Don't worry," I said as I reached for her hand.

"I'll drop you off at the medical center on time and then go to Jessica's house and make sure she is all right." I backed out of the driveway and headed down the street.

We were almost to the main highway when Maury turned to me with tears in her eyes and said, "Jessica's friend, Heather, just called. She wondered if we had talked to Jessica today. She hasn't heard from her since Saturday and they were supposed to make plans to go shopping today after my appointment." She sat back and stared at the street ahead. I felt an uneasiness creep into my stomach and up my spine. We drove in silence the rest of the way.

"I'll call you as soon as I talk with Jessica, so don't worry." I kissed Maury goodbye and backed out of the parking space at Memorial City Medical Center. She turned and walked to the door, stopping only briefly to wave and wipe tears out of her eyes. I could see the fear on her face clearly from my vantage point, and I knew it had nothing to do with her appointment. Over the years, Maury has had more than her share of medical issues and some of her treatments had been rough. But in everything she had been through, I had never seen that look and it unnerved me. *God, please calm her spirit and mine too.*

Turning the car around, I headed to Jessica's house. She lived about thirty minutes away from the Medical Center but that drive felt like eternity.

My mind ran ahead as my thoughts began to race. They swung back and forth between, "Oh God, protect our baby" and "I'm going to kill her if she is languishing in bed."

As I drove down her street, I saw her car in the driveway and my stomach began to churn. "Please, God, let her be okay," I prayed. "Let her be asleep. Let her be sick, but let her be okay."

By the time I parked and jumped out of the car I was in full panic mode. I ran to the porch and began to bang on the door. I could hear her dogs barking inside. They should have been out in the backyard by now. Something was definitely wrong. *Maybe she is sick or hurt and can't get to the phone.*

"Jessica, open up," I yelled as I pounded. The dogs came to the door when they heard my voice and began to whine. Climbing through the tangle of bushes in front of her living room window, I bent down to pick up the spare key she hid under a rock for those times when she misplaced her keys. She had a habit of laying them down in the weird-est places. One time she found them on the edge of the bathtub. Another time she found them in the refrigerator. She never remembered leaving them in those places. We used to tease her about having a fairy who carried her keys off when she wasn't looking.

I brushed the dirt off the key and wiped my hands on my pants. Unlocking the front door, I stepped in. "Jessica," I called. All was quiet except for the dogs' incessant whining. I took them to the back door and let them out. They stepped outside but immediately turned to come back in.

Something was very wrong. I slammed the door before the dogs could run back in and stood, frozen in place, afraid to move. I looked around the room but all was in order. A few glasses were on the coffee table, a few pillows on the floor. *Nothing out of the ordinary.* Things looked okay. But somehow, I knew they weren't. I called out to Jessica again but all was silent. Bile rose in my throat as I struggled to breathe. "Oh God, help me."

I walked toward the kitchen hoping to get some answers but not wanting to see what they were. A half-empty wine bottle and an empty pizza box on the counter. *Nothing unusual here.* Jessica loved pizza, just like her mom. She didn't care if it was warm or cold, just as long as it came from her favorite restaurant, Antonio's. Many nights she would call in an order, throw on her sweats, pour a glass of wine, and veg in front of the television while she waited for dinner to arrive.

I turned and headed slowly toward the stairs that led to her bedroom, calling her name softly with each step. Dread filled my heart.

With leaded feet, I climbed the stairs, stopping briefly at the landing, and called Jessica's name once again. When no answer came, I pushed on. It felt as though I was wading through quicksand. My heart was racing, yet my legs felt so heavy. Reaching the open bedroom door, my heart stopped.

"Oh God. Oh God," I cried. "Jessica!"

She lay face down on the middle of the bed. The sheets and blankets were pulled back in a tangle of color. She wore her favorite blue nightshirt and her golden hair was splayed over the pillows she lay between. I dropped to my knees and pulled her into my arms. "Jesus," I breathed. "Help us!" Her skin was so cold and much paler than usual. *No, No, No! This cannot be happening.* I struggled to breathe.

I pulled my daughter's body off the bed and laid her down on her back. I couldn't make sense of what I was seeing. Her lovely face was all bruised. There was blood coming from her nose. *Who would do this?* Her eyes. Those beautiful eyes were open and she was looking up at the ceiling. But she wasn't seeing the ceiling. She wasn't seeing anything. My precious baby girl was gone.

What do I do? Get help. Get help!

I looked around for a phone. Funny how the mind fails to work when you are in the middle of a crisis. My thoughts felt fuzzy and my brain was moving in slow motion. Finally realizing I had my cell, I pulled it out of my pocket and punched 911. I held the phone to my ear. "Help," my brain screamed. But I remained silent as the ringing continued. Finally, I heard, "911, what is your emergency?"

"Help," I whispered. "Please help my daughter. I think she's gone. She's not breathing."

The voice on the other end of the line was irritatingly calm. "Sir, how do you know she is not breathing?"

The room began to spin and all I could do was whisper, "Help my Jessica."

Chapter 2
The Princess Arrives

I MET MAURY THROUGH mutual friends over thirty years ago. I really wasn't looking to marry again. It hadn't worked out the first time around.

When I was seventeen, I was on top of the world. As a senior, I was quarterback of the school football team and dating the head cheerleader. I was headed to graduation and then to college. Coming from a small town, I was considered a "golden boy" with a bright future.

One Friday night my girlfriend Liz and I went out for pizza. As she slid into the booth across from me, she gave me a funny look.

"What?" I said as I reached for the menu. "What do you think? You up for pizza supreme tonight?"

"Steve," she said quietly as she laid her hand over mine.

I put the menu down and looked at her; *really*

looked at her.

"What's wrong? Are you okay?"

She withdrew her hand, looked down for a moment before whispering in a desperate voice, "Steven, I think I'm pregnant."

The world stopped for a moment before I could absorb what she said. "Okay, we'll figure out what to do," I replied, not sure what I even meant. And that was how I proposed to my first wife.

We married a month later with our parents' "blessing." Then we graduated high school and I went to work. College was no longer an option. I was a family man from then on.

Liz didn't feel well during her pregnancy. She had lots of nausea from the beginning. It was a stressful time for two kids to be trying to put a life together. I was exhausted all the time from trying to provide for both her and me. And, I was terrified I wouldn't make enough money to support our baby when he or she arrived, so I took every opportunity to work overtime.

Liz was resentful of my being gone such long hours and my lack of attention toward her. I had never had to pay bills before and resented that my hard-earned money had to go to keeping the lights on when I should have been using it for fun while at college. After all, I had worked hard in high school to keep my grades up, and I should have been enjoying the freedom of college life. I began to see our situation as more her fault than mine.

Needless to say, things went downhill pretty fast. We descended into a pattern of yelling, crying, accusations, name calling. It was pretty miserable, but we stuck it out for the "good" of our baby.

They say hindsight is clearer than the present, and unfortunately that seemed to be true, at least in my case. When I looked back, I could see Liz was just a scared kid dealing with a lot of shame and fear. And I was just a jerk.

But when little Joy arrived, and I held her for the first time, I was in love. Really in love. I would do anything to keep her safe and cared for. It must have been hard on Liz to watch me be so open and loving toward our child and yet so closed off from her as my wife. Our marriage limped along for three long years before we finally called it quits.

It was the most painful decision I'd ever had to make. To walk out of Liz's life and leave my daughter behind was excruciating. Divorce can be traumatic and having come from a broken home, I didn't want that for my child. I didn't know at the time that God could have healed our relationship if only we had been willing.

I spent the next few years randomly dating, afraid to get "stuck" in another bad marriage. So, when my friends told me about Maury and what a fabulous woman she was, I wasn't really interested. I was building my life around work and weekends with my child, and was just fine without the hassles of a relationship. I didn't have the time or energy to invest in anyone or anything else. Maybe later, but not then. My friends, though, were persistent and to get them off my back, I finally agreed to meet Maury for lunch.

Later, I found out she'd felt like I did. Having come from a bad relationship of her own, she was done with men but to be nice, she'd agreed to meet. When I saw that blonde beauty walk into the restaurant that day, my heart did a flip-flop. This was the woman my friends had set me up with? Why had they waited so long to get us together?

We had lunch and then instead of going our own ways, like I had planned, we sat at the table and talked. I found out she loved children, pepperoni pizza and walks in the park. I learned she was very close with her aunt and uncle. We talked on and on until the waiter started giving us dirty looks, then I put a hefty tip on the table, smiled at the waiter and escorted Maury through the door. We crossed the street and walked through the park where we sat on a bench and talked some more. I couldn't explain it, but talking with Maury was like "coming home" in my heart. The memories of so many bad relationships from the past began to slip away, and I had hope of a possible future with a woman to share in it.

I came from a strict military family. My parents had divorced when I was five and my childhood had been quite chaotic, being shoved back and forth between angry adults. My father hadn't been the nurturing type, and as a young boy, I was sensitive of spirit and really needed a mother to care for me. Since she was not a part of my life for years, I grew up tough to cover the hole in my heart. It wasn't until I was older that I realized so many of my poor choices were the result of me looking for unconditional love in the form of a woman. Little did I know the only one who can love like that was God. But when I saw Maury walk in the door, I *knew* I had found "the one."

Maury had two older brothers and two older sisters. As the baby of the family, her siblings were very protective of her. They were great people but wary of anyone she dated. I was in pretty rough shape when we met. A typical twenty-three-year-old single man, I smoked and drank and caroused around, but the more I got to know my beauty, the more I wanted to be a better man. But how to accomplish that was beyond me.

The wonderful thing about Maury was that she loved me exactly as I was. She saw through my tough veneer and quickly took me home to meet her family. I was nervous and didn't want to screw things up. I really cared about this girl. So, wanting to make a good impression, I dressed as nice as I could and was on my best behavior. What a surprise it was to find her family were just as accepting of me as Maury was. They never treated me as an outsider. As time went on, Maury's siblings began to realize we were in love, and so they accepted me without question and welcomed me into their family. I would often go over to her eldest sister and brother-in-law's house and help Don with the yard work while Maury and Bev cooked dinner. The four of us would eat and then spend the evening watching television together. The love that was shown to me during our times together started to soften me. Slowly I began to grow into a man I could be proud of.

One night, while driving Maury home from Bev and Don's house, after an evening of cards, she told me to pull over so we could talk. I felt uneasy but did as she asked. *Was she tired of me? Did she want to date others?* I could see in the moonlight she was struggling with something.

Being one who was given to speaking her mind, she looked directly at me and said, "Steve, you know I love you dearly, but I can't marry you."

My head began to spin and I thought I would throw up. "What? What are you talking about, Maury? We are destined to be together." I felt desperate to convince her of what seemed so obvious to me.

"When I was a young girl, I had a terrible accident and I can never give you children," she quietly replied. She had tears in her eyes and her face reflected such pain.

I reached for her hand, looked into those big blue eyes and said, "Maury. That is no big deal to me. We have each other and that is all I need." *And*

I'm already a father. I have my little girl, Joy.

"But it's every man's dream to have a house full of children," she continued.

"No, Maury, my dream is to share a house with you." We talked late into the night and Maury finally began to see we *could* have a rich and full life without having children of our own.

We were married the next year in Bev and Don's backyard. It was a beautiful ceremony made even more special having taken place at the home of a family who had shown me a path to wholeness. God's hand was working in my life at that time even though I was so unaware. My in-laws provided the unified family I had never had. In marrying Maury, sinking into their lives and soaking up all their love and acceptance, God began to heal the wounds of my past.

Life was full and busy. We had it all. I was starting to make money and during the week when Joy was with us, we were a snug little family who did everything together. We went to the movies, to church, on picnics—anywhere and everywhere we could as a family. And when Joy was with her biological mom, Maury and I would go out and party with friends.

I thought I had finally "arrived." After all, I had a wonderful wife, a loving child, friends and money. What more could a man want?

One night, while getting ready for bed, Maury told me she was feeling somewhat incomplete. Typical for a man, I gave her all the reasons why her feelings were silly, and listed everything that made her life full. I had no clue what was wrong with my wife, but I somewhat naively figured she was just being an emotional woman. It wasn't long before she approached me again. This time her words got my attention. "I want to adopt a baby." She didn't ask my opinion or seem to want to discuss her idea. She had made up her mind.

Maury was strong and tenacious that way. Every time I tried to explain how perfect our life was and how we had decided before our wedding we didn't need more children to make us a family, she dismissed my words. Maury was going to "upset the apple cart," no matter what I said. She began to research adoption agencies and in our nightly prayers she started asking God for the little girl she knew He had waiting for us. She prayed for our future baby and after a few months, I began to warm to the idea. If it would make Maury happy, why not add to our family? After all, my job was going well and I was making a decent living. Nothing much would change for me with another child in the home. Maury ran that ship. So, as my heart began to change, I joined in the prayer for the new little girl who was out there somewhere.

One night after work as I drove into the driveway, I saw Maury standing in the doorway. She had an excited look on her face. I knew something was up but could not fathom what it could be.

"Steve," she said as I got to the door. "Guess who I talked to today?"

"I have no idea," was my reply.

"I talked to my mother and guess what?"

"Okay, Maury. I can't guess, so why don't you just tell me," I said as I plopped down on the sofa, weary from a long day at work.

"Well," she said smugly as she sat down beside me and took my hand. "You know my mom runs a boarding house and is always asking God to bring her those who need to be cared for."

I nodded for her to go on with her story. "She has a single mom living in her basement who can barely pay the rent," she said excitedly.

"Get on with it, Maury," I said. I was getting impatient and wanted to take my shoes off, eat dinner, and watch television.

"Oh, Steve. She's pregnant, but her boyfriend wants nothing to do with her and has run off. And she is struggling to keep her one child fed and doesn't know how she is going to care for another infant. That poor girl needs help."

I shifted in my seat as I said, "I don't see what that has to do with us. I'm sure your mom will take good care of her."

"No, Steve. You don't get it," she said. "My mom called to tell me the poor girl is thinking of giving her baby up for adoption and she is considering us as potential parents."

Now she *really* had my attention. "Slow down, Maury. I'm not so sure about this. Have you really thought this through? It is awfully sudden."

Maury let go of my hand and looked me straight in the eye. *Uh oh*, I thought. I'd seen that look before and no matter what I said, the deal was done. Maury was already mothering this new child in her mind and heart. So, what could I say?

I realized there was only one way to approach this. In the last few years I had grown closer to the Lord, and I knew if it was His will for us to have this child then we needed to seek Him. So, I grabbed Maury's hand and said, "Let's pray."

And that was what we did.

Soon it became apparent that adding another child was God's will for our family. The pregnant young woman that Maury had told me about, adored Maury's mother and was so happy to know her baby would have a good "Christian" family and an opportunity for a wonderful life. By now, Joy was with us full-time. Her mother was struggling and decided to move, so to help Joy with the transition and make her feel a part of this venture, we told her she could name the new baby. She spent considerable time on this project and ultimately decided on Jessica. Joy and Jessica. That worked for me. And to honor Maury's godly mother, Mary, who had started the ball rolling that brought Jessica to us, we gave her a middle name of Mary.

Five months later, I received a call at work. It was from Maury and her voice was excited. "Steve! Jessica is on her way," she'd practically shouted into the phone.

"What? Where? What?" I asked, totally confused.

"She's on her way. Jessica is on her way. Mom just called to say Trish is in labor."

While I felt a sense of excitement, I am a somewhat cautious person and needed to be reassured that this was right.

"How do you know this baby is to be ours, Maury?" I quietly asked.

"I just *know,* Steve. When I heard my mom's voice, I had such joy and I heard in my heart, 'Jessica is your daughter. She will be yours from today.' I have no doubt that was God's voice."

I had learned over the years to trust Maury when she said she'd heard from God. And so, we got in the car and headed out to adopt the little unknown baby into our lives.

Soon we were waiting in a private room at the hospital for the arrival of Jessica. After four cups of stale coffee and what seemed like an eternity of pacing and sitting, and pacing some more, the door opened and in walked a nurse with a tiny bundle. I was on my feet immediately.

"Here she is, Daddy," the nurse said with a smile as she handed the bundle to me. One look into those deep blue eyes staring at me from inside the pink blanket, and it was exactly the same as I had felt with Joy. I was in love. Amazing how that happened. There was no difference between my birth child and this child. She was my daughter. No matter how she came into our family, she was ours. As I stood staring at our precious baby, I was suddenly struck anew by the words of apostle Paul in Galatians chapter four, when he said that Jesus paid the price so that we could be "adopted as God's sons." So, the moment I accepted Christ, Romans chapter eleven said that I was "grafted onto the family tree and started growing into the likeness of that tree, Jesus."

According to Ephesians chapter one, I have the same right as a "birth child" to run to my Father for comfort, protection, and grace. I will receive the same inheritance as those who are His chosen people, the Jews. And best of all, I am now called His child because He chose me to love. Just like we chose Jessica.

This was the first of many gifts I received from Jessica: a deeper understanding of God's love for me. This little one, who wore a pink knitted cap and had a little wisp of white hair sticking out, burned into my soul how deep and incomprehensible God's love was for His children.

"My princess, my beautiful little Jessica. Thank you, God, for sending her to us. What a gift of love," I cried.

My wife looked on with a smile as I stood there cradling our new daughter while tears slid down my face.

"Let's take our princess home," she said.

•••

I opened my car door, got out, and went around the car to help Maury and the baby out, but I had to stand in line. Joy was already straining to take Jessica out of Maury's arms.

"Slow down, girl," I said to Joy. "Let Daddy carry your baby sister."

She backed up enough for me to reach in and lift that little bundle out of the car. We paraded into the house carrying the one grafted into our family tree.

Our house became filled with baby stuff. A crib, a playpen, a walker, a highchair, baby blankets, bottles, toys, burp cloths, pacifiers, tiny clothes, diapers-so many diapers. The list went on and on. Every room had paraphernalia required for the new baby. I had forgotten how much necessary equipment arrived with the entrance of a new little one. Our house was stuffed to the gills. It was messy and cluttered, and felt full and blessed.

Friends and neighbors helped celebrate Jessica's arrival with an outpouring of gifts. My co-workers even threw me a "Daddy Shower". With all the generosity of others, our once comfortable, organized house began to shrink. So, for the next few years, I happily dodged blankets on the floor, stepped over (and on a few) toys as I made my way through our living room and out to work each day. And when I came in at night, no matter how difficult the day might have been, Jessica would always be at the door, with a big smile on her face and arms raised for a hug. Joy was a young teen by then but still greeted me with love and affection each night, and it was nice to know I was the center of their worlds. I knew that would pass as they grew up, so I soaked up every sloppy kiss and sticky hug given. Maury was often right behind the girls as they greeted me at the door, and her smiles of approval and warm hugs completed my welcome home. I was at peace.

Chapter 3
School Days

TIME PASSED QUICKLY WHEN you were raising kids. One day Jessica was a baby and the next day I turned around, and she was skipping out the door to go to school.

She was a beautiful child. People would stop me on the street to comment on her looks. Hair the color of spun gold, porcelain skin, and deep blue eyes that sparkled all the time made for much conversation with strangers whenever we went out. Our little Jessica was bright and a bit precocious. And she knew her mind.

When she was about three, I took Jessica to the grocery store with me while Maury was busy elsewhere. In those days, stores often had child-sized merry-go- rounds, and the one in front of this store had three little horses on it. Jessica spotted it, let go of my hand, and raced toward the ride. She climbed up on the first horse she came to and begged me to "Make the horsey go, Daddy!" How could you resist a request like that? I deposited a quarter in the slot, and round and round Jessica went. She shrieked in delight. Watching the expression on her little face, I stood there, grinning from ear to ear.

After the end of the ride, I heard, "Again, Daddy, again!" So, I fished in my pocket, found another coin, and around she went again. The look in her eyes told me Jessica was imagining being off in a meadow somewhere, riding like the wind on a big white magical horse.

I don't remember how many turns she had that day but I do remember when I ran out of change, and how I was finally able to pry her off the horse and continue our errand. Little did I know, Jessica was destined to one day have a big chestnut-colored *magical* horse of her very own.

Jessica loved animals, especially horses. Her room was a warehouse of every kind of toy horse there was. The walls were covered with pictures she had drawn and posters we had purchased, all of horses. From a very early age, she checked out every equine book the library had. She was an avid reader and began to acquire a huge amount of knowledge about her passion. She became especially interested in jumping horses.

One day, Jessica's best friend, Heather, came over to play. I could hear their happy six-year-old chatter in the other room as I did paperwork in my home office.

Suddenly, I realized things were very quiet, so I laid down my pen and softly walked to Jessica's bedroom door for a peek. There they were, Heather with a rope around her neck, being the horse, and Jessica leading her around in circles, and teaching her how to jump over the blocks they had laid on the floor. From that point on, the only *horse* Jessica was allowed to lead around by a leash was our family dog, and then only when an adult was supervising.

We have always tried to give our girls opportunities to be involved in what they enjoyed, so it seemed fitting to give Jessica riding lessons. She was thrilled and loved the lessons, but soon she wanted a horse of her own. She badgered me constantly to take her to look at one horse or another but my answer was always the same. "It's too much responsibility for you," or "Too much money" or "I just don't have time." That didn't deter Jessica from her dream though. She changed tactics and approached the subject again.

When she was about eight, Jessica came to the breakfast table early one morning and quietly sat in her chair. That was not her normal behavior. She was usually cheery and talkative when she woke. She didn't touch her food but just sat, staring out the window.

"What's wrong, honey? Don't you feel well?" Maury asked.

"No, I don't feel good, Mommy," Jessica answered.

Maury felt her forehead. "Well, you don't have a fever, but why don't you go back to bed and I'll call the school?"

"Yes, Mommy," Jessica replied and she dragged herself back to bed.

A little while later, Maury heard the phone ring.

"Hello," she answered.

"Is Jessica there?" a woman's voice asked.

"Who is this?" Maury asked with a bit of suspicion in her voice.

"My name is Abby Foster and Jessica left me a message about purchasing one of my horses."

Maury began to laugh. I'm sure the woman on the phone was very confused why Maury sounded unfriendly at first and then suddenly started laughing.

"Jessica is only eight years old," she cried between fits of laughter. "That little stinker pretended to be sick today so she could wait for your call."

The poor confused lady said she was sorry, but Jessica sounded much older than eight and she knew a lot about horses. They chatted a little while longer before hanging up the phone.

That night, after some stern words from her mother and I about calling other adults without permission and lying about being sick, Maury and I tucked Jessica into bed and went to our room.

"Now what?" Maury asked. "What do we do about getting Jessica a horse? She *is* beginning to win competitions and you know her trainer has said several times that Jessica is so good, the only reason she tends to take second place is that she is out-horsed."

We talked long into the night and finally decided that maybe purchasing Jessica a horse of her own would be worth the investment. So, Jessica got her first horse. And as predicted, she began to win competitions all over the country.

We hired a great trainer, who really knew how to draw the best out of both horses and their riders. But over time, I began to hear from the trainer, "Jessica is being out-horsed again."

So off to Germany they went: Maury, Jessica, our trainer, and two other moms.

It'll be a nice vacation for my girls. They will see some horses and go sightseeing and that will be it. Little did I know they would come back with a commitment to buy a very expensive horse.

I had to admit, Ascona was a fabulous horse. She was a beautiful chestnut-colored Trakehner mare who stood 16.5 hands high. Jessica adored her, and together they proved she was worth every hard-earned dollar.

They made a great team. The two of them began to take grand champion as a hunter jumper everywhere they went. And at each event, once Jessica won, little kids would flock to her side and ask for her autograph or to have a picture taken with her. She was always patient with them, and stayed put until the last child had their questions answered and their requests granted. She loved kids and I'm sure she recognized those who were destined to be winners like her.

The downside is, Jessica seemed to be somewhat accident-prone. She was well known at the minor emergency. She had several falls and broke her ribs a few times, but she was tough as nails. Sometimes, I didn't even know about her injuries until they healed.

When she neared eighteen, Jessica began to ask to have surgery on her eyes for her myopia. It seemed like a reasonable request and it should have gone smoothly, but after the first surgery, my tough-as-nails daughter began to complain about intense pain in her eye. Maury and I became alarmed because Jessica was not one to cry easily, and she was crying a lot. So, in we went to see the surgeon.

After the initial examination, we were told Jessica was allergic to the stitches in her eye. So back we went for another surgery. This time they removed the stitches and once healed, Jessica was back, asking to ride again. The girl never gave up on anything she believed in.

In total, Jessica had five eye surgeries. This, unfortunately, left her without depth perception, which was a death knell to a horseman. You needed good eyes for the sport. But true to her nature, Jessica tenaciously retrained her eyes, and once finally corrected, she was back on her horse and we moved forward.

While horses were everything to Jessica, she also threw herself into anything that touched her spirit. When she was eight, we took her and her friends bowling. It was lot of fun and I didn't think much about the day, other than how enjoyable it had been watching the kids enjoy themselves. They bowled a little but spent most of their time eating chips, drinking soda, and getting treats from the candy machine.

Two days later, Maury received a call from the school nurse.

"Mrs. Branson," the nurse said. "This is Susan Corley from Jessica's school. She came in to see me this morning with some disturbing news that I wanted to discuss with you."

Maury later relayed to me how the nurse's first words made her feel concerned. But the disturbing news was not about our daughter; it was about what she had seen at the bowling alley.

"Our school is taking part in the *Great American Smoke Out*," she'd said, "and Jessica told me anyone can buy cigarettes from the candy machine at the bowling alley."

This wasn't a huge surprise to Maury. During

those days, people were unaware of the dangers of cigarette smoking, and there was no law about how old you needed to be to buy them or smoke. The nurse referred to the first step in a program regulating the selling of cigarettes to minors.

"Jessica is such a bright and articulate little girl," Nurse Susan told Maury. "I wonder if it would be okay if she worked with me on the project."

Maury assured her that if Jessica was interested, it would be okay with us. We had no idea what was coming.

That same year, Jessica and one of her friends were the youngest persons to testify before the state senate about the evils of making cigarettes available to children. Their testimonies resulted in passing a law that prohibited selling cigarettes in candy machines. Yep. That girl had spunk.

By the time she spoke to the senate, I had gotten myself together spiritually and was really trying to walk with Jesus and become the man He wanted me to be. So, I was reading my Bible daily to grow as a Christian. We were also going to church regularly and praying at our dinner table. Jessica went to Sunday school and went through confirmation class at our church. She accepted Jesus into her heart at that time and began to read her own Bible.

She was an astute reader. By fourth grade, she was reading at high school level, so it should not have surprised me that she actually read through the scriptures seven times in her short life. I was so impressed that this young woman drew on her tenacity to read the whole Bible, and not just a verse here and there like so many of us did. It began to show in her life and others started to ask her to pray for them for various situations. She was always happy to do so.

Jessica was a good student and graduated valedictorian from a private high school in our area. She had a multitude of friends and was always busy with them. Vivacious and outgoing, she had the unique ability to accept everyone as they were, without judgment. She had a caring heart and was always helping someone.

Maury had become seriously ill, and it was Jessica who attended to her most of the time when I needed to be at work but didn't want to leave Maury alone. Maybe that was why she decided to become a nurse.

She and her mom talked daily, and even though she was in school and was still busy riding and being with friends, if she sensed a need in her mom, she dropped everything to care for her.

I still believe she would have been a fabulous nurse since she could handle pain yet was compassionate to others when they were in a season of suffering. And she did seem to have that sixth sense about how others were doing. Maybe that was why so many people counted on her to pray for their needs.

Chapter 4

Descending Into Hell

"HELP MY JESSICA!"

"Sir! Sir!" The 911 person took command of the situation. "What is your address?"

The address? I didn't know. I couldn't think.

"I have to go look," I said, and ran out of the room, stumbled down the stairs, and made my way outside to read the numbers on the house. I had been to that house a million times and was good with numbers, but nothing would connect in my brain.

"4307 Melody Lane," I said into the phone.

"Okay," the voice said. "Now, sir. I am patching you through to EMS. Hold on one moment."

The other line was silent for only a few seconds when a male's voice spoke. "Sir, do you know CPR?" the faceless voice asked.

I nodded my head yes, as if he could see me.

"Start CPR, sir. Do you hear me?"

"Yes, yes, I can do that," I replied.

"Good. The ambulance is on its way and I'm staying with you until they arrive. You can do this. I'm here with you."

It was strange that I needed such direction at that time. I was a self-made man with a take-charge attitude. I had built my own business and provided well for my family. But my brain was mush as I covered my daughter and began doing compressions on her.

I didn't hear them come in, even though it seemed like forever before they arrived. While my arms hurt so badly from the repetition, I couldn't stop. I kept working, tears running down my face, snot running out my nose.

"Come on, baby. Come on, baby," I desperately cried.

That's when I caught a glimpse of a figure out of the corner my eye and glanced over my shoulder. There were several EMTs standing there, quietly watching.

"Can't you do anything?" I cried.

"No, sir. I'm sorry," one of them said quietly and with obvious compassion. "Let us take care of her now."

Standing up, I walked to the bathroom, blew

my nose, and wiped my eyes. Trying to fully comprehend that this was real, one thought kept coming to my mind: *How do I tell my Maury that our sweet Jessica is gone?*

One of the EMT workers came to the bathroom door and asked me to go into the other room so we could talk. I shuffled down the stairs and into the living room but couldn't sit. Instead, I leaned against the doorframe and tried to concentrate on his questions, answering everything as best as I could.

Standing there, trying to think, I glanced around the room.

"Hey, where is Jessica's television?"

"Television?" the EMT asked.

"Yes." Suddenly my mind went razor sharp. "She has a big-screen TV and it hangs right here." I pointed to the big blank space on the wall.

"Does she have another TV anywhere in the house?" the EMT asked.

"Yes, in her room."

My head began to spin. What in the world was going on? It can't be that someone hurt her, hurt my little girl, just to take her television. Her dogs would have protected her. None of this made sense.

"Brad," the EMT yelled to someone upstairs. "Is there a TV in there?"

"Not in here," was the reply.

The EMT turned to me, a different look on his face this time. "Sir, you better get out of the house."

"Why would I do that?" I asked.

"Because this may be a homicide."

•••

Outside I went. I hadn't realized until then that the fire department had sent a truck along with the ambulance. Lights were flashing on both vehicles. I wondered why the fire truck was there. It seemed so out of place without a fire. But nothing was making sense, anyway.

I could see people looking out their windows and slowing down as they drove by. To avoid talking to any of them, I got in my car. I wasn't sure what to do, but I did know one thing: the fewer fingerprints I left in Jessica's house, the better chance the police had to find the fingerprints of the killer.

Killer.

What a word. It went hand in hand with victim. To be a killer you had to have a victim. And this evil person, this son of the devil had one—and it was my daughter.

Rage rose in me. I suddenly wanted to pay back the one who murdered my child.

Maybe not kill him or her. That was too easy. But I sure wanted to make them suffer. Suffer the way Jessica had.

But did she suffer? Was she afraid? My thoughts

ran wild and I thought I would suffocate under the possibilities.

Yanking the car door open, I got out, desperate for some air. Pacing up and down the driveway, I knew I couldn't leave. What would I tell Maury?

Maury! Oh God I've got to get to her before she shows up over here. And she would. As fragile as she was, and as ill has she had been those last few years, she'd crawl out to the car if she felt the need to get to one of her children or grandchildren.

I hated not being able to be the one to tell her our youngest child was now with Jesus. We had been through so much heartache together over the years, it didn't seem right to have her face the news without me there. But I didn't have a choice. I couldn't leave until the police arrived.

So, I decided to call Joy. But before I did, I called our granddaughter, Jaime. She was attending the local college, and I knew she'd be happy to skip class to pick her grandmother up from her doctor's appointment and take her home. Jaime was such a loving girl and would drop everything to help.

I called her and tried to sound as cheerful as possible, telling her I was hung up at work and needed her to take Maury home. She happily agreed, even when I told her to make sure and tell her grandmother I was doing the errand Maury asked me to do, and I would call her soon. Then I hung up and made one of the hardest phone calls of my life. Calling Joy.

Joy had always been a happy person. Even as a child, when her mom and I broke up, she weathered that storm with faith and trust. And during the years when she lived with her mom and a series of Liz's boyfriends, she kept a positive spirit and moved forward.

She came to faith as a young girl, but now she was a mature woman. Deeply committed to Christ and extremely sensitive to others, I knew she would be the only other one I could trust to share this news with Maury.

She and Maury were very close. They had never really been stepmother and stepdaughter. From the beginning, Maury embraced her as her own and Joy reciprocated.

Dialing her number, I sent up a prayer that I would be clear and that Joy would know exactly what to do for Maury.

"Hey Dad, what's up?" I heard her cheerful voice.

"Joy, what are you doing right now?" I asked as nonchalant as I could.

"I'm in Belmont baking Christmas cookies with a friend. Why? What do you need? Is Mom okay?"

Suddenly my mind went muddled again. "Joy," I stumbled, "your sister, Jessica, she's gone."

"Gone? Gone where, Dad?" she asked.

My tears began again. "She's gone. She's dead. I found her. The police are coming. Your mother—"

"Dad!" Joy cried. "Slow down! Jessica is dead? What are you talking about? What happened?"

"We don't know for sure but we think someone did this. I can't go home yet. Please go tell your mom for me and *don't* bring her here. Keep her at home."

"Okay, Dad. I understand. Don't worry. I'll go home and I'll take care of Mom. I love you, Dad. Jesus be with us," I heard her breathe as she hung up the phone.

I paced back and forth until my emotions settled somewhat. But all I could do was get back in the car to wait some more. What was taking so long?

Some of the EMTs came out and stood around their ambulance. Some stayed inside with Jessica. One stopped to ask if he could do anything for me and suggested they check me out since I had been through such a traumatic event. I thought that was ridiculous. *If they couldn't help Jessica, they sure couldn't help me.* But he was persistent, so I relented.

Getting out of the car, I walked up the driveway and climbed into the ambulance. Someone hooked me up to a monitor that took my pulse and temperature and then they checked my heart. For the most part it was all a blur, but eventually I noticed a small crowd of neighbors gathering. One of them recognized me and called from the sidewalk.

"Are you okay, Mr. Branson?"

"I'm fine," I returned.

The EMT turned around and smiled at the young man as if to affirm that I was okay. But I knew I would never be okay again.

I was kind of glad for the buffer of vehicles and the "official" personnel. There was no way I could talk to anyone at that moment. I kept swinging between numb and being overcome by emotion.

Once they decided I wasn't going to have a heart attack, I got back into my car to be alone and wait for the police who were supposedly on their way.

It took them over an hour and a half to show. I watched people drift by. Some looked very suspicious to me: gawking at my daughter's house but avoiding eye contact with me. *Was one of them the murderer, returning to the scene of the crime?*

"Don't you worry, baby," I promised Jessica. "I won't ever give up until he is found and punished for what he did to you."

Little did I know it would take years to fulfill that promise.

Chapter 5
Stumbling Through The Dark

I WATCHED AS TWO police cars drove up and several officers emerged from their squad cars and headed to the house. One of them wasn't wearing a uniform and he headed straight to the EMS crew. He spoke with them briefly and, as I got out of my car, he turned and walked toward me. Meeting me on the lawn, his first words were, "Are you Mr. Branson?"

"Yes," I answered, starting to feel weary.

He extended his hand toward me and I took it. It was a strong hand, one that looked as worn as I felt. He was an older man, impressive in height and size. He had a commanding presence but a kind voice.

"Mr. Branson, I'm Detective Kestner, from the homicide division. Let's go inside so we can talk."

I followed him into Jessica's living room, sat

on the couch, and simply stared at her Christmas tree. It wouldn't be long now before the lights would come on and the tree would sparkle and shine. How odd to sit in such beauty while feeling such horror.

"I am sorry for your loss, Mr. Branson." The detective interrupted my thoughts.

I turned and thanked him.

"I would like to ask you a few questions if you are willing."

"Of course," I said.

I could see through the front window that a small crowd was gathering outside the house. I was glad the police wouldn't let anyone in.

Other officers were wandering around the house, opening doors, snooping in closets, taking pictures. It was distracting.

"Mr. Branson?"

I looked back at the detective.

"Tell me what happened."

He pulled out a small notebook and flipped it open. *Just like on television.* This was all so surreal.

"Jessica was supposed to pick up her mom this morning and she didn't show," I said quietly.

Suddenly the bedroom door opened, and I saw them carry Jessica down the stairs and past me. She was strapped down and was covered from head to toe with a blanket. Feeling a surge of energy, I jumped to my feet.

"Take that blanket off her," I commanded. "She won't be able to breathe!"

They ignored my outburst and kept going. Except for Detective Kestner. He stood up and put his hand on my arm.

"We'll take it from here, Frank," he called to the men with the stretcher. And with that, they walked out with my little girl and shut the door.

I sat down in defeat. "Where are they taking her?"

"To Memorial Hospital," came the answer. "What is your daughter's full name?" he asked.

"Jessica Mary Branson," I replied. "She was named after her grandmother."

His next words were, "Spell it please."

How cold and sterile the questions are. My daughter is dead and you want to know how to spell her name? It was too much to absorb all at once.

I spouted off the spelling of her name and then stared at him.

"Continue with your story," Kestner said.

"My wife has pancreatic cancer and had major surgery recently. She had an appointment with her doctor this morning, and Jessica was to take her. When she didn't show, Maury, my wife, was worried about her so I came over to see what was up. I thought maybe she was sick or something, but not this." Tears began to run down my face again.

"Okay, I need you to sit here and fill out this report. Just write down everything you remember," said the detective in response to my explanation.

I struggled to write. The memory of Jessica's body burned into my mind. To this day, I can still see every detail of that scene. Yet so many details of the rest of the events of that day are fuzzy.

I wrote and thought and cried, and wrote some more. Finally, when I could not think of another word to put on the paper, I got up and walked into the kitchen where a few cops had congregated. Detective Kestner was with them so I handed him the paper.

He took it and asked if I was able to drive home or if I needed someone to take me. I assured him I could drive.

"Okay, Mr. Branson. You go home for a few hours and be with your wife. But come back at"— he looked at his watch--"ten tonight so we can record your statement."

How weird, I thought. *I just wrote down everything I could remember and I need to go home and see my wife.* So why on earth he would want me back that same night was beyond me. But I obliged him and after thanking him for helping my family, I walked out the door to my car and got in, totally ignoring those thrill-seeking, nosy neighbors still present.

Turning the key, I heard the engine roar to life and without making eye contact with anyone, I drove down the street, turned the corner, and headed home.

Truth was, I wasn't sure how I really got there. I was suddenly so tired and my thoughts were so jumbled, I wasn't totally conscious of where I was going, or the surrounding traffic. But God graciously delivered me to my front door. I couldn't wait to see Maury and yet I dreaded seeing her. I knew she would be in terrible emotional pain and I wasn't sure how much the stress would affect her body. She had just had major surgery six weeks earlier and was so fragile.

Pulling up in the driveway, I saw that one of our garage doors had been bashed in, as if someone had rammed their car into the door. Was someone out to hurt my family? Did that someone kill Jessica, and then come here and do this as a warning to Maury? Did anyone have a grudge against me and I didn't know it?

The day before, I would have stormed into the house and demanded to know who had caused the damage, but that night I barely glanced at it as I raced by. I needed to get to my family and protect them.

Maury was standing in the open door before I got to the front porch. Her face was puffy from crying. She fell into my open arms. I stood there clinging to her, glad to finally be close. We had always drawn strength from one another and this time was no different.

The world faded away. We were alone; no one else existed except us. After a few minutes of absorbing each other's strength, we pulled apart from our embrace and moved into the house, closing the door and the rest of the world out of our lives for now. But we kept physical contact. I had my arm around Maury and as we walked into the living room she quietly asked, "What happened? Tell me."

I led her to a chair and waited until she settled before I said anything. I heard whispering behind me. Turning, I saw Joy and her husband, Rick, sitting on the sofa. It took me a moment to realize they were holding hands and quietly praying for all of us and for God's leading during this time. Joy opened her eyes, got up, came over to me and hugged me tight.

"I love you, Daddy. God will take care of us." She pulled away, looked me in the eyes, and returned to the sofa.

We sat in our living room together as a family and I shared all I I had seen and everything I knew so far. It was getting dark outside, yet it felt as if time was standing still. It was hard to think and easy to cry. There were more questions than we had answers for. We felt helpless, unsure what to do next. No one mentioned dinner. We just sat.

Joy and Rick were beside each other talking quietly about how to tell their kids about Jessica.

"Crap. I forgot the dogs," I said. "I put them in the backyard this morning and forgot about them. I bet they are hungry and panicky. Jessica would never leave them out so long."

"Don't worry about them, Steve," Rick said. "I'll go get them and take them to my mom's for now. She won't mind. You know how much she loves dogs."

How did I get such a wonderful son-in-law? He was so good for Joy. He loved her and the kids and was so good to us. He was truly a godsend to this family.

Rick pulled out his phone and punched in his mom's cell number as he walked into the kitchen. I couldn't hear exactly what he was saying but could tell she was asking all kinds of questions to which he had no answers. He returned soon with an, "It's all set. She says to tell you she is so sorry about Jessica and to let you know she is praying for us. She said I can bring the dogs over any time and they can stay as long as needed."

Remembering I had to go back at ten to record my statement, I told Rick he would have to wait until I went back since I didn't think the police would let him into the house to get the dogs. Meanwhile, Joy phoned her friend and made arrangements for the children to spend the night so she could stay with her mom while I went back to Jessica's. As all this happened around me, I looked at Maury. She was pale and exhausted.

"Come lay down," I said as I moved toward our bedroom. I didn't know how long it would take to give my recorded statement, and I wanted to make sure she could rest while I was gone.

"Yes, come on, Mom," Joy said. "I'll lay down with you while Dad and Rick go take care of things."

Maury looked at Joy then at me, sighed, and got up. I put my arm around her thin shoulders, and walked her into our room with Joy following behind. Putting Maury on the bed and propping pillows behind her, Joy went to get slippers for her feet. Maury was often cold since her surgery and needed to keep her legs and feet covered. Joy asked if she could bring us something to eat or drink, but we both declined. Joy was determined, however, so while I sat with Maury, she went into the kitchen, brewed tea, and made several pieces of toast. Soon she was back with the food, and a bowl of ice cream, just in case Maury couldn't swallow toast. So thoughtful that daughter of mine.

Laying everything on a tray table, Joy got on the bed and crawled over near her mom. She grabbed Maury's hand and sat quietly. I got down on my knees beside my wife, reached for her free hand, and began to pray. I thanked God for Jessica's life and for Joy and Rick and our grandchildren and especially for Maury, my life partner.

I thanked God for the police who were going to find this monster who had killed my daughter.

I asked God to protect them and bless them for doing their jobs.

And I asked God to protect the rest of my precious family.

After saying amen, I stood. I touched Joy's hand and kissed the top of Maury's head before turning around to go. Rick was standing in the doorway, quietly waiting. As I walked to him, he backed up to give me room to go by. But I grabbed him and embraced him.

Tears flowed again, but Rick stood there holding me. How grateful I was for such a strong, Christian man in my family.

Rick was a quiet, unassuming young man, but I had come to know him as "Quiet Thunder." He was kind and gentle of spirit but you couldn't mistake that for weakness. Underneath, he was strong and would go down fighting for what he believed was right. He stood for his God and led his family in ways I'd never even thought of when I was his age. He was full of wisdom and courage. I couldn't have imagined a better man to stand beside me in that time of raging grief.

Heading into the night, I led the way to Jessica's, and Rick followed in his car. On the way,

I began to think about Detective Kestner, and the rest of the police who were in Jessica's house. I had no idea when their day started and how long it lasted. I figured most of them had families just like me. Many would be waiting at home for them at this late hour. I wondered if their wives ever got used to the late nights of being without their spouses. And how did they deal with the fear of their loved ones possibly not coming home from work one day? Funny, I never thought much about it before. I took for granted the police were there to give me speeding tickets when needed and help me if they saw me stuck on the road with a flat tire. And of course, I knew they would come if I called 911 in an emergency, but what about the awful things those men and women saw every day?

Those images would haunt me. I honestly didn't know how they could stand in the gap between good and evil on a daily basis and still function. Those thoughts gave rise to a new awareness that everyone of faith in our nation should pray daily for our law enforcers. And that night began a new routine for me. Daily, I thanked God for my family and asked God's protection on them, but now I always added prayers for those who protected us and for their families who allowed them to do so.

I rounded the corner to Jessica's street and the fire engine and the EMS truck were gone. But several police cars were still there. And someone had put that yellow police tape around the front porch. The door was open and policemen were still going in and out.

Parking my car in the driveway, I got out, Rick pulling up behind me as I waited for him. Together we walked past the taped-off area and into the house.

Detective Kestner met us at the door. I introduced him to my son-in-law and explained he was there to get the dogs. The men shook hands as Rick thanked him for being there for Jessica.

The detective stopped, looked at me, and quietly said, "I have a daughter of my own." He then cleared his throat and returned to the business-as-usual persona I had met a few hours earlier.

"Mr. Branson," he said. "How is your wife?"

How do you think she is? But it was kind of him to ask so I told him she was resting at home and that my daughter, Joy, was with her.

Rick looked around at the police who were still milling around inside and headed out the back door toward the dogs, who were barking again. They must have recognized him, because I could hear them whine and jump around happily when he opened that back door. He shut the door behind him, but I could still hear him, pulling the lid off the metal can that held the dog food. He was talking to the dogs as he worked. I was so grateful for Rick, taking that responsibility off my shoulders. *That's one less thing I have to worry about.* Soon all was quiet as the dogs were eating. Now I could concentrate on the task before me.

Detective Kestner suggested we sit at the kitchen table for the recording of my statement. I went to the coat closet, pulled out the dogs' leashes and took them to the back door to one of the officers.

"Please give these to my son-in-law and tell him not to wait for me. I'll meet him back at the house," I told him.

He nodded, and I turned and followed Kestner into Jessica's kitchen. There was the pizza box and the wine bottle still sitting on the counter. Walking over to the table, I sat while the detective cleared the room.

He placed a small tape recorder on the table and turned it on. Speaking into the mic, he said, "December 15, 2012"—he looked at his watch—"21:37. This is the recorded statement of Mr. Steve Branson."

Chapter 6
Making A Statement

I'D BEEN INSTRUCTED TO speak slowly and clearly, and to take my time while being recorded. Detective Kestner officially asked me to tell what happened that morning .

I repeated everything I could remember. After the trauma of finding Jessica ten hours earlier and the fatigue of the day, my mind was a bit jumbled, but I did the best I could. The detective asked a few detailed questions along the way. The interview only lasted only about thirty minutes, but in some way, it felt like it went on forever.

"Thank you for coming back and recording your statement, Mr. Branson," Kestner said.

I nodded. "Now what?"

"You go home and wait. We will take it from here. We'll be in contact."

So that's it? I thought. *I go home and sit on*

my hands until someone calls me and tells me they caught the guy? No way. I made a promise to Jessica and I intended to keep it. I was going to do everything I could to help the investigation and was committed to bringing the person who did this terrible thing to justice.

Trauma is a strange thing. Everyone feels urgency in the beginning, and then the world begins to return to a normal pace so those who are suffering the most are being told to go home and wait. But the adrenaline doesn't stop for the suffering. It keeps pumping for a long time, which makes waiting nearly impossible. That's where I was at-trying to settle down enough to wait.

I thanked the officer, shook his hand, and told him I was on board to help in any way. Then I headed home.

Rick's car was already there, so I knew the dogs had been cared for.

As I went inside, Joy came out of the bedroom followed by Maury. I hugged each one as we walked into the living room and flopping down in the first available chair, closed my eyes.

"Here, Mom," I heard Joy say. "Lie down on the sofa. You'll be more comfortable."

"I think I will," came Maury's weary voice.

We sat in our living room together as a family and talked about the events of the day. It was dark outside, yet many of the neighbor's yards were lit up with Christmas lights and yard ornaments. Our Christmas tree was on, too. It was the only light in the room.

It felt as if time was standing still. Surely, it should be morning by now. We all had so many questions and we shared them there in the darkened room.

Lost in thought, I heard Maury's voice quietly float across the room.

"I crashed into the garage door," she said.

"I know," I replied. "I'm just glad you weren't hurt."

"I couldn't wait any longer, Steve," she explained. "I *knew* it was the worst when you didn't answer your phone."

"You don't have to explain anything to me, Maury," I said as I got up to go to her. Sitting up, she made room for me on the sofa so I could put my arms around her. "None of that matters. We are together right now, that's all I care about."

We sat in silence for a few moments, then I began to chuckle.

"What?" Maury looked up at my face.

"Well, I feel silly saying this but when I saw the garage door, my first thought was maybe someone had a grudge against me or my business, and was after my family and they did that to the door to let me know they were after me."

Joy began to giggle. "No, Dad, it was just Mom. When we drove up, she was coming down the street, so Rick pulled in front of her and blocked her car. I jumped out and got in with Mom and told her about Jessica. You know she actually backed her car down the street past three houses before roaring up your driveway?

I thought she was going to drive us right into the kitchen. It was a bit of a wild ride!"

We all had a brief moment of comic relief picturing Maury's car zooming backward down our street.

The moment was short-lived. It got quiet again until Rick spoke up.

"You know, God has incredible timing. After you called Joy this morning, she immediately called me and asked me to come and pick her up. She didn't trust herself driving from Belmont after hearing about Jessica. It took me about forty-five minutes to get there and forty-five back. If Maury had left five minutes earlier, we would have missed her. But God knew exactly when we needed to be there to help. Isn't that amazing?"

As I looked back, I could see that was the first of many things God orchestrated for us during this journey of night. He put Rick and Joy exactly *where* they needed to be, exactly *when* they needed to be there. He had my grandsons at a friend's house so they weren't in the middle of it all. And he kept Maury from seeing what I saw, for which I am eternally grateful.

It was near midnight when we all parted. But before Joy and Rick left, we stood and held hands as I prayed. I thanked God that Jessica was safe with Him and asked Him to take care of her until we get to heaven. I thanked Him for Joy and Rick and for my Maury. I asked Him for the right words for Rick and Joy when they told our grandkids, and I asked for wisdom and strength for the days ahead. I finished and then listened as Rick spoke to the Lord. And then Joy. And then Maury.

We were all sobbing as we hugged goodbye for the night. But while our hearts were broken, I realized our spirits were at peace. That was such a gift from God. Knowing that no matter what, He loved us, He loved Jessica, and He was with us moment by moment on this dark path. The knowledge of that truth was more than comforting. It helped strengthen us for the days ahead.

Psalm 119:5 said, "Thy Word is a lamp unto my feet and a light unto my path." A lamp only illuminated a few feet ahead on a dark path and maybe it was better that way. If I could have seen the events coming knowing I couldn't have stopped them, I would have dropped dead on the spot. But now all I was able to do was hold His hand and carry my lamp as we walked this dark road together.

Chapter 7

Putting The Pieces Together

MAURY AND I LAY in bed beside each other, but we didn't sleep much that night. Every once in a while, the silence would be broken by one of us saying something about Jessica and her time on earth with us. Then there were more tears. We spent most of the night alternating between talking, crying and praying.

"I want to go to Jessica's house tomorrow," Maury's voice came through the dark.

"As soon as it's light, dear, as soon as it's light. We aren't sleeping anyway so we might as well," I answered as I patted her hand.

Suddenly, the dawn began to filter through the curtains. I guess we must have drifted off for a few hours. Glancing at the clock, it was a little after 5:30 a.m. I looked over at Maury. She was breathing evenly and didn't stir as I got out of bed.

Heading toward the kitchen to make coffee, I thought about the day. We had an appointment with the funeral home at 11:00 a.m. Joy would meet us there.

I sighed as I waited for the coffee to brew. "God," I said out loud. "Why did you take our baby girl home so soon? She had so much living to do. She should have had time to become a nurse, find a good man, marry, and have a family. Why now, why so sudden, and *why this way?*"

My spirit felt weary, as well as my body. Even though I didn't understand God's plan, I was glad I could lean into Him for comfort and strength, even if He didn't give me the answers I wanted.

I heard the shower going as I headed to the bedroom with two cups of coffee in my hands. I guess Maury wasn't sleeping so soundly after all. Laying a mug on the bathroom counter and heading back toward the living room, I sat down in my leather chair and opened my Bible.

The Psalms had always been such a comfort to me in the storms of life. This was definitely a major storm that had blown through our lives, so I turned to Psalm 139:11-12.

"If I say, surely the darkness shall cover me, and the light become night around me, even the darkness is not dark to you; the night is bright as the day, for the darkness is as light to you," I read.

"This is true, Lord," I prayed. "None of this is a

surprise to You. This dark valley of the 'shadow of death' is as light to you. You see the way. Lead us."

Turning the pages, I found another familiar verse. Psalm 55:22. "Cast your burden on the Lord, and He will sustain you, He will never permit the righteous to be moved."

I prayed again. "Lord, here is our burden of grief. You promise to sustain us and keep us stable. I trust you."

I didn't get a chance to finish my prayer. Maury came in dressed and ready to go. I looked up just as she said, "You better get ready for the day."

After I showered and shaved, we headed to Jessica's. It was still early and all was quiet in her neighborhood, which I was glad for. After seeing the spectators standing around watching the police go in and out and knowing they saw Jessica being carried away, I didn't want to see anyone. I didn't want to answer any questions.

When we drove up to the house, I saw an envelope taped to the door and something on the stoop, but couldn't quite make out what it was. As I headed to the door, Maury followed right behind me.

There on the welcome mat sat a plate of cookies with a note attached. The front simply said, "Please accept these cookies as a gift of care and concern from one of Jessica's neighbors."

Maury picked up the plate and pulled the card off the door to open. It was a sympathy card. Someone named Sue wrote "Mr. and Mrs. Branson, I am one of Jessica's neighbors. I saw her being carried out yesterday. I am so sorry. Jessica was a nice young woman and was well liked in this neighborhood. We will miss her. Please know we are praying for you during this terrible time of loss."

I could hardly see the words as my eyes filled with tears. The kindness of strangers moved me. Suddenly the spectators of yesterday became the caring neighbors of that day. I stood convicted of my own judgmental attitude. What would I do if I were in their shoes? I would probably be first in line to watch but would I pray for them? Would I find a way to show concern for them?

Maury voice broke into my thoughts. "Let's go in, honey."

Slowly, I unlocked the door and we stepped in. It was eerily quiet.

Looking around the room, I couldn't help but notice there in front of the window was Jessica's Christmas tree, all decorated with crosses and angels. She loved angels, always had. Angels I knew she was with now, because of Christ's sacrifice on the cross.

My thoughts were so clear. The way to live eternally among the angels was simply through Christ. Nothing more; nothing less.

Maury and I walked through all the rooms. Jessica's bed was just an empty mattress where she had lain, probably because the police had taken the blankets to test for DNA. It looked so bare and sterile, like a motel room being stripped clean for the next person to use. I didn't want to see it anymore.

So, I went into the kitchen. The pizza box was still there. *Were we supposed to take it out to the trash?* I didn't know why, but that struck me as funny. Did I think the police were going to take care of those things? Didn't I realize we were to take care of it all now?

Get it together, man, I thought. Of course, I will take care of this. That is what dads do. They take care of their family. So, I picked up the pizza box to carry it out but Maury called me from the living room.

"Steve, where is Jessica's purse?" she asked.

I walked back to her and looked around. Funny, I hadn't noticed it wasn't hanging on the coat closet doorknob where she always kept it.

"I don't know," I answered. "I don't remember seeing it yesterday. Surely the EMTs wouldn't take it, would they?" That didn't even make sense. "Let me think a minute," I said. But I had no answer, so I headed to the kitchen, picked up the pizza box, and went into the garage to throw it away.

Lost in thought, I lifted the lid on the trash can and stepped on a cigarette butt. I looked around and noticed several on the garage floor. Jessica did not smoke and never had. After speaking before the state senate on keeping cigarettes out of the hands of children, she'd always felt strongly about the dangers of smoking. Something wasn't right.

I picked up one of the butts and carried it inside.

"Maury, look at the this." I held it up for her to see. Her eyes grew wide. "I'm calling the police. I need to make sure they know these aren't Jessica's and they might be a clue as to who was here that night."

Shivers ran down my spine as I began to feel alarm. Her killer had been all over her house. She must have known him.

"I better call Detective Kestner. But let's see if anything else is missing first."

Since I now knew Jessica's purse was gone, I knew they had her keys, her phone, and her garage remote. So, while Maury walked to Jessica's room, I went to the garage. I had moved Jessica's mustang into the garage yesterday so I was relieved to see it was still there, right next to the '79 El Camino I had restored.

The first thing I did was unplug the garage door opener so whoever those people were, couldn't come back and add insult to injury by driving away in our vehicles. To think of them joyriding around made me feel sick, and I felt a small satisfaction in knowing I had probably thwarted their future plans to return for more loot. I made a mental note to call a locksmith to change all the locks to the house.

Back inside, I found Maury sitting on the edge of Jessica's bed, looking at the bloody mattress. She was running her hand over it, almost like she was petting it. Then she climbed up on the bed and lay down where Jessica had been. I'm sure it made her feel close to our daughter. So, I stood quietly watching her as she closed her eyes and lay there.

After a few minutes, she sighed, opened her eyes and got up. She fluffed up the pillows and patted the mattress. Then she turned to me and said, "They took her jewelry. All of her beautiful jewelry." And she walked for the door.

"Wait!" I called after her. "All of it?"

"Yes."

Evil, wicked people. Jessica loved bling and she wore it well. She liked expensive things and worked hard for them. One of the rings was worth a lot of money and if the killer was as dumb as I hoped, he would try to pawn it and that might lead the police right to him.

I was so angry at the thought that someone would take Jessica's life and then take his time to systematically strip her of anything of value to cash it in for his pleasure, that I felt more motivated than ever. *He won't get away with what he did to my daughter.*

"I'm calling the detective," I said. "I've got new information him."

Chapter 8

The Funeral

OUR NEXT STEP IN this nightmare was to plan our child's funeral. Something NO parent should have to do, no matter how old their child is. It is so out of order. We raise our kids and launch them into the world when they are ready to take care of themselves. Then we feel a bit of relief that they will be okay when we are gone. But this… this is SO wrong. Maury and I drove to the funeral home in silence. I pulled into the parking lot and turned off the motor. We sat quietly in the car for a few moments, looking at the large red brick building before us. I couldn't believe in a few days we would meet our daughter there one final time, and lay her to rest in the cemetery behind.

Maury sighed. I looked over at her, the love of my heart, strength of my life. She looked so weary. I knew this was heartbreaking for her, and was unsure how much more she could take. She was so ill and I was worried about her, both physically and emotionally.

Reaching over and gently rubbing the back of her neck, she looked at me and gave me a sad, sweet smile.

Taking her hand, I said, "Well, are you ready, honey?"

"I'll never be ready for this," she replied.

"Dear Lord, help us," I whispered in desperation, and opened the car door. Just then Joy drove up beside us. I was so glad she was there, as I knew she would be good support for Maury during such a distressing time.

The three of us walked to the oak door together. Holding it open for both women, I then followed them into a thickly carpeted foyer. It was well lit and full of sofas and chairs placed in little groups of three and four. I assumed it was for the grieving to sit and chat with loved ones.

All was quiet in the expansive room. We weren't there but a few moments when a door close by opened quietly and a tall man dressed in a suit and tie came out. He came directly to us and extended his hand.

"You must be the Bransons," he said, shaking my hand. We nodded in response. "I'm Fred Pollard. I'm sorry for your loss."

"Thank you," I whispered.

"Let's go into the conference room where we can talk privately," he said.

Putting my arm around Maury, I held her close as Fred led us into a small room with a large table in the center. There were leather desk chairs all around the table, and in the center was a large binder. Next to it was a legal pad and two pens.

For some reason, I took in every detail, even though compared to the loss of my daughter, it was completely irrelevant.

He offered us chairs and seated himself directly across from us. I sat between my two loved ones. Being close to both my girls made me feel more anchored.

Mr. Pollard opened the binder to the back pages and said, "Mr. and Mrs. Branson, we have here some elegant styles for your loved one to rest in."

His voice was kind and soft, but the conversation rubbed me the wrong way.

"Her name was Jessica and these are coffins," I said in response.

Everyone went silent. I'm sure Mr. Pollard was used to dealing with people like me, people wracked with grief who could hardly think. And yet, his job was to help people make decisions they didn't want to make.

"Of course," he said quietly. He folded his hands and placed them on the binder. "How can I help you, Mr. Branson?"

I wanted to cry. I wanted to scream. I wanted to jump up and run out of that building and keep on running. I wanted to wake up from this nightmare. But I sat quietly for a moment and then said those dreaded words.

"We need help planning our daughter's funeral."

Mr. Pollard remained gentle and kind-hearted, despite my initial outburst. He led us through the maze of planning Jessica's "Celebration of Life," as he called it.

The details all ran together. We picked the date and set up who would sing, who would read scripture, and what the order would be. Joy took notes because obviously she knew I couldn't keep track of the information.

Finally, we went through the dreaded binder: the binder of coffins. It should have been an easy decision, but we couldn't agree on any of the elegant styles in his book. None of them seemed right to us. So, we sat.

Mr. Pollard finally suggested we look at their custom order options.

Maury suddenly spoke up. "That is exactly what we will do. We are picking out one that will represent Jessica's life. It needs to be right."

So, we did. We ordered a beautiful casket and had it embroidered with an equestrian rider on her horse, jumping fences. It looked like Jessica. Pure.

Elegant. Strong. Free. It was perfect.

After several exhausting hours of decision-making, we thanked Mr. Pollard for his help as we got up from the table and shook hands. We also promised to get pictures of Jessica to him for the slide show sometime the next day. Once again, Joy stepped in.

"Don't worry, Mom," she said. "I'll take care of the pictures."

We each got into our respective cars, Joy waved as she took off to do errands and to work on the pictures. Maury, on the other hand, was exhausted. It had been a long morning. So, I took her home so she could rest.

Convincing her to lay down, I fixed her a sand-wich and carried it into the bedroom so I could lay beside her. We didn't talk, and it was good to be quiet together. Peaceful within our darkness.

Later that afternoon, there was a rap on the back door followed by Joy's sweet voice.

"Knock, knock," she called. I heard her come through the kitchen.

"We're in here," Maury called back.

"Hi, I just came by to get some more pictures of Jessica for the slide show," Joy said. I could hear her move into the living room and move things around on the bookcase.

Sitting with Joy while we went down photo

memory lane, I started thinking about all the people we needed to call about the funeral. Joy and I made a list. She took a lot of photos, some memorabilia to set up, and the list. I honestly didn't know how we would have gotten through those dark days without her attention to detail, tireless energy, and even though her heart had to be broken as well, her strength. I felt so blessed by her love and constant compassion for us.

Saturday would be the day of the funeral, and I knew I wanted to speak. No, I needed to speak. I hated what was done to my daughter, but God had been speaking into my heart, and I knew I could not spend my life hating the one who ended my daughter's life. I needed to focus on the good things, like the children and grandchildren we were blessed with. I felt compelled to make clear the message God had given me, and with His strength, I knew He would give me the words to speak.

•••

We planned on a public funeral and burial.

Burial. Such a final word. We had all attended funerals and all knew that after the burial, it was over. Friends and loved ones stood around the gravesite for a few moments to hug the grieving and say a few words of comfort but ultimately, they walked away and gave the family a few moments to say goodbye.

What a tragic scene that was. We didn't want it

to be that way. We wanted Jessica's "Celebration of Life" to be just that. We wanted to focus on the gift she had been to us and how thankful we were for the twenty-six years God had loaned her to us. More importantly, we wanted to share how God had and would continue to sustain us.

We had already said goodbye to Jessica the night before she left this earth. We just didn't know what a gift that was at the time.

It was December 14th, and Joy had invited the whole family to attend her church's nativity scene. Her older son was one of the shepherds. It was the first time he was in a play, and he was so excited. Given it was an outdoor event and it was cold, Maury and I bundled up. Maury was still recovering from a nine-hour surgery she had five weeks earlier, but I knew she wouldn't have missed seeing her grandson be a shepherd. That was one thing about Maury that amazed me. No matter how bad her health was, she never missed an opportunity to be with family. I admired that little woman's stamina in the midst of serious medical issues that could take a grown man down. She was a powerhouse.

Before we left, I had texted Jessica to remind her of the time and told her we were leaving and would see her there. She lived forty-five minutes way so we knew opportunities to see her niece and nephews were sometimes limited.

Arriving at the nativity with coffee cups in hand, we watched as our grandson played his part beautifully. He looked up at us once and smiled with pride. Jessica arrived shortly after we did and we stood together as a family, enjoying the event. When it was time to go, we all hugged and said our goodbyes. In hindsight, I'm so grateful we had the habit of saving we loved each other as we parted, and thankfully, that night was no different.

Like always, because she was single, Jessica would text me when she arrived home. That night, at ten thirty, she texted that she was home safe and finished off the text with "I love you."

That was the last message I'd ever read from my sweet princess. Little did I know within twelve hours I would find her gone from our lives. My heart ached.

●●●

Saturday arrived and we were up early. I'm not really sure Maury or I slept much the night before. I'm not sure we had slept much since the nightmare began seven days ago.

Absorbed in our own private thoughts, all was quiet in our house as we got ready. Maury showered and dressed while I spent time with the Lord in my chair. I was nervous but not afraid. I wasn't concerned about proclaiming God's grace in our lives. I was even somewhat excited about that part. I was nervous about making sure I could remember what I wanted to say when standing in front of a crowd.

Maury emerged from our bedroom looking tired but as always, lovely. I took my cue and headed toward our room to get ready. There was no guideline written on how to prepare for your child's funeral so I wasn't sure I knew what I was doing. I thought I'd practice my talk while shaving, but realized the only thing my brain would say was "Lord, help us today. Help us today."

Really, what else was there to say? Without the Lord's help, we wouldn't have been able to stand up to the stress and grief. We wouldn't have been able to survive this nightmare. We often wondered aloud about how people who didn't know Jesus got through things like this. It was still a mystery to me.

When it was time, Maury and I headed to the funeral home. When we arrived, the parking lot was already beginning to fill. Once we'd found a spot, I breathed a prayer for us.

We held hands as we walked to the same door we had entered earlier in the week. Walking inside, we were greeted by Joy and Rick, who had come earlier to help with last-minute details. Rick's parents would bring the grandkids later.

Mr. Pollard was also present and led us to a private family room, where we could settle until time for the service. *Settle.* How could we settle? It was horrible to be there and even though it was a comfortable room, with boxes of Kleenex on every table and bottles of water close by, I wished we were anywhere but there. Mr. Pollard told us we could have some time alone with Jessica and led us to another room where she lay in her coffin.

We stood together over her body and wept. Maury ran her hand over the embroidery on the coffin. It truly was lovely. I touched Jessica's long hair and was flooded with memories of the first time I saw her with her little tuft of hair sticking out of her pink knitted hat.

The four of us held on to each other, murmuring things like, "She looks beautiful" and "Rest now, sweet girl." I led my family in prayer and thanked God for every day of Jessica's life. I also asked His blessing on me for when I would stand in front of those who had come and speak of His love for all. Then we went back into the family room to wait. Soon our grandchildren joined us.

Before long, we could hear people gathering in the foyer. The noise grew and grew and I realized a lot of people had come. Family members began to arrive and as each one entered our private room, I would stand to greet them with a hug. After a few words, each new attendee would take a seat to wait with us. Our pastor arrived to pray with us. But we simply sat cocooned in our room, until Mr. Pollard entered and told us to line up in a certain order with Maury and me at the front.

As we filed into the small chapel, I saw the pews were filled. So many people had come to honor us by celebrating Jessica's life with us. It was almost overwhelming.

We settled into our seats and the sweet strains of Carrie Underwood singing "How Great Thou Art" flowed through the speakers as the slide show began. It was such a bittersweet experience—to be swept away into pictures of Jessica from her birth to her last days on this earth.

At the end of the montage of pictures, our pastor stood and spoke. He shared a few stories about Jessica and how she'd loved Jesus. He spoke of God's love for us. I couldn't remember everything he said that day, as my mind felt fuzzy and not much else penetrated the fog. When my pastor was finished, I hobbled up to the pulpit on crutches, which understandably, surprised many. Once there, I set them aside and stood before our friends and family to share my heart.

"I am not in need of crutches today," I said. "I brought these up because they remind me of Jessica. She was always getting hurt—usually during practicing jumping her horse. It seems like she was in the emergency room every month or so, but she never complained. And she never gave up. She was tough, and yet she was tender of spirit. Jessica always wanted to help others. Once, when Jessica was four years old, she and I were walking on a sidewalk along a busy street. I made her walk on the 'inside.' Like all little children, she asked me why. I explained I walked on the side close to the street so I could protect her. She stopped walking, let go of my hand, looked up at me and told me she wanted to walk on the 'outside' to protect *me.* That was Jessica. Always looking out for others. When she grew up, she stood with her mom by her aunt Bonnie's bed as she took her last breath. With a heart so keen to help others, she was going to school to be a nurse. Jessica never let anything stop her."

I took a deep breath and continued, "You know, if you are riding a horse and you come to a *jump*, you have several choices. You can stop before it, you can go around it, or you can jump. Jessica always jumped. And now . . . now she has jumped into eternity." They were some of the hardest words I spoke that day.

I said some other things but before I sat down, the song "I'll Fly Away" was played. It was hard to listen to the words and focus on what I wanted to say, as my heart was breaking again, picturing her face as she flew away. Jessica had ridden away to heaven, and after sharing that with those who gathered, I prayed. I asked God to please help the police catch the criminal who murdered my daughter. I asked God to make sure he was prosecuted to the full extent of the law. And I asked God to please show the man who ended Jessica's life on earth the way of salvation so he would not spend eternity without the Lord.

We ended the service with those in the pews filing up front to walk by Jessica's casket. It was strange to watch the reactions of people as they walked by. Some people paused, touched, and wept. Others simply looked as they passed.

As I watched, I heard the Spirit say to me, "Don't miss this, Steve. See how people react. This was the same way they reacted to the gospel. Some looked and *talked* about God and how good He was. They said He loved everyone. *And He does.* But that was where it stopped. No personal investment in any kind of relationship with Him. Others simply looked quickly at the spiritual side of life, but kept on walking. They stayed busy in life so they didn't have to deal with their need for a savior. But then there were those who stopped, took a good look and wept. They wept in repentance for the sin in their lives and then they wept for the joy of salvation. *Don't miss it, Steve. I want all my children to stop, weep, and bow before Me. I want them all to realize I long for a relationship with them, and I will do anything to reach them."* It begged the question: What would we do with the fact that Jesus died for our sins, and then rose from the dead? It deserved a response in everyone's lives.

Chapter 9

Missing Pieces

ON MONDAY MORNING I went to Jessica's house to meet the locksmith. I had some time to kill while he worked, and was feeling less angry at the neighbors, so I started knocking on their doors and asking if anyone had seen anyone or anything that might be helpful.

One man happened to be up early and said he saw a silver Honda pulling out of the driveway at 5:30 a.m. the morning of Jessica's death. It was the first solid clue. Immediately I thanked the Lord that this man had to work that early. Then I made a mental note to call the detective with the information. That was until the neighbor said the police had been there after I found Jessica. They already knew.

I used to watch those crime shows and try to figure out who committed the crime and why. It must have affected me more than I realized, because I looked at everything and everyone with new eyes. I scrutinized our entire world. I thought about the case constantly to the point of obsession.

Taking inventory of all that was missing, I realized the total value was roughly $21,000. That was enough to be booked as a third-degree felony in our state. To me, it looked like things were beginning to fall together.

I started calling Detective Kestner whenever I thought of something to *help* him in the case. He always returned my calls and listened to my ideas and answered all my questions. Every time I spoke with him, I thanked him for caring. I couldn't believe he was so invested in our situation. I also let him know that many were praying for him. I think that touched his heart to realize he was more than just a man doing his job; to us he was the man God was using to vindicate Jessica.

I started thinking about who Jessica had talked to on her last day on earth. So once again I called the detective and asked if he could somehow get the missing cell phone records. His reply shocked me.

According to him, when the police requested records, it could take up to forty-five days to get them. No wonder things moved slowly. He suggested I try to get them, because he believed I could get them faster since I didn't have to go through "official" channels like he did. So, I did.

It took a lot of phone calls and talking to lots of

people before I finally found the person who could actually help me. And help me he did. I received the phone records for the entire year.

And what do you know. On the morning of December 15th:11 a.m. was a call to my girl from a number in a town close by. There was also a record of several texts from the same number. I wanted to call it back but knew I needed to trust the authorities that God had brought into our lives to do what was needed. I requested a transcript, but was told that unfortunately, cell phone companies no longer kept those records.

Christmas came and we did all the things we normally did. We bought and wrapped gifts for our grandchildren. We finished decorating the house. We went to Christmas Eve service at our church. But nothing could lift our spirits. The sadness of our loss permeated the entire holiday season. Everything felt…less, with Jessica gone.

Moving into the New Year was tough. We took down our decorations but I could hardly bear putting away Jessica's tree. I knew the time had come, but it had somehow been a comfort knowing her tree was covered with angels watching over her house. Maury and I discussed it and decided to go undress the tree together. So, we got in my car and drove to Jessica's.

We stopped the car in front of the house and sat for a few minutes. The house was dark, just like my mood. I helped Maury to the door, unlocked it and entered. Maury had not been there since the day she discovered Jessica's purse was missing so I wasn't sure how she would feel being back. The house was quiet as we walked into the living room. Everything looked the same as the morning our nightmare began. The silence was deafening. Maury sat on the couch and watched me as I plugged in the tree. I joined her and we sat in the darkened room and stared at the beauty of the angels glistening in the tree lights.

"I wonder what she is doing tonight," Maury whispered in the dark. "Whatever it is, I'm sure she is giving it 100%," I replied.

We continued sitting with my arm around my beloved wife for a long time. Finally, I got up, went to the closet and returned with the ornament boxes. Maury and I spent the next hour slowly removing the evidence of Jessica's last season on earth. The murderer had taken away our family Christmas but he would never take away our hope of someday celebrating Christ's birth together again.

Chapter 10
Miracles Appear

FEBRUARY ARRIVED AND TIME seemed to drag. Oh, it was so hard to wait on the Lord, and resting in Him was so difficult. But I did know He was with us on this journey and was leading Detective Kestner every step of the way.

It had been two months since Jessica's death and life continued. February 21st was Jaime, my granddaughter's birthday. We planned on celebrating at a favorite restaurant of ours. It was going to be a bright spot in an otherwise dark road we'd been on. So that night we dressed up and headed out for the evening.

Maury and I talked all the way there about how fast Jaime had grown and what a lovely young woman she was becoming. But in chatting about old memories, the conversation kept circling around to Jessica and the fact that she should be celebrating with us. Talk about bittersweet feelings.

Jessica had been a great aunt. Having no children of her own, she took every opportunity to spoil her niece and nephews. She relished in celebrating every holiday and knew how to make a party out of the most mundane accomplishments. Win a writing contest? Celebrate with Aunt Jessica. Get one hundred percent on a spelling test? Make sure you call her because she would take you to McDonalds for fun. Jessica spared no expense when it came to birthday presents, and I knew our grandkids loved to get gifts from their aunt. Jessica adored children and it felt like a terrible loss that she'd never get the opportunity to become a mom, because she would have been fantastic at it.

We met Joy and her family in the parking lot and after hellos and hugs, walked into the restaurant together. We were seated immediately and the banter was light and carefree. It was good to look around the table and see those I loved enjoying themselves. I realized we were all making an effort to keep the "normal" in life while we lived in this abnormal time, but I kept seeing in my mind's eye that empty space where Jessica would have and should have sat. I reached under the table and squeezed Maury's hand and she responded in kind. We smiled at each other and focused on Jaime and *her* special night.

As hard as it was to push the feelings of grief out of my mind the for the night, it was good to celebrate the lives of those who were still with us. It was good to know we hadn't lost that perspective.

No doubt I had God to thank for that revelation.

Later that evening as we parted from the others and climbed into our car, we waved as Joy and Rick drove away. I heard my phone ding and assumed it was Jaime saying thank you for her gifts. She was such a sweetheart that way. Instead, I was stunned. *Speechless.*

Looking at my phone, I saw a text from Jessica's number.

I looked over at Maury who immediately knew something was wrong.

"What?" she asked.

"It's from Jessica's phone," I whispered. And I began to read out loud. "Are you missing a phone?"

What in the world was this? I thought. Who had her phone? Was it the killer playing a sick joke on us?

I was afraid to ask for fear they would stop texting, so I said, "Yes, I am."

The person texted his phone number, and said he was presently out of town in Wallace, about five hours away, on business but would be back in a few days and would make contact to give me Jessica's phone back. So many questions were going around in my mind, but two things were most prominent. How did he know to contact me? Did he know about Jessica's phone since December? If so, why contact me now?

Of course, my mind began going through all the scenarios. Maybe he found it or bought it at a pawnshop. Maybe he was just a cruel person who wanted to mess with me. I didn't know, but I was willing to take any chance to help with Jessica's case.

I told the "texter" I would be happy to give him a reward.

His response was, "No thanks, a reward isn't necessary. I just wanted to get the phone back to its owner."

After more conversation, he informed me that he had found it about twenty miles from our home in a ditch by a major highway. He said he was walking along and saw something shiny in the grass so he picked it up, wiped it off, and decided to take it home and see if he could get it to work.

We'd had so much rain in the last two weeks, I couldn't understand how he thought it would be salvageable, but he had. Being that he worked in telecommunications, he was able to locate a charger that fit Jessica's phone

Of course, I didn't tell him why I needed the phone for fear he would change his mind and disappear. Instead, I just thanked him for his generosity and handed the phone to Maury. As we headed home, Maury and I talked about how clearly we could see God's hand in this turn of events.

I could hardly wait to talk to Detective Kestner, so I called him early the next morning. He was surprised by my story, but assured me he would send someone to Wallace immediately and would get back to me as soon as he had the phone in hand.

I spent the rest of the day trying to work, but my eye was on the clock and my mind was on any and every scenario. Maybe the police showed up and he was gone. Maybe the man lied about where he found the phone. Maybe he had changed his mind and pawned the phone. Finally, I gave up on being productive and went home to wait with Maury. Thank goodness Mike was still pulling his weight as my manager, and was used to taking over for me when my brain couldn't focus anymore.

I was only home about fifteen minutes when my phone rang. It was Detective Kestner.

"Well, did you get it?" I practically shouted into the phone.

"Yup," he replied. "Phone in hand and the texts are intact. And they show who she was talking to in the early hours of the morning of her death."

Chapter 11
Miracles Abound

THE RODEO CAME TO our area once a year and it was a huge event. We had always loved going, so for all the years our girls were growing up, we were heavily involved. I served on the rodeo committee and had a display set up for my business each season. We also had box seats for every performance. It was such a fun time for our family to go and watch the cowboys, bull riders, and the many other performers. Jessica, of course, particularly loved the horses.

We attended every performance we could and then took the kids to the fair grounds to ride the rides. We would eat hot dogs and funnel cake, and indulge the girls when they begged for stuffed animals and other trinkets. What great memories we had of those years. As the girls got older and more independent, we would allow them to use our tickets to take their friends and dates to the rodeo. They both loved treating people to the event, but there were times Maury and I missed the family tradition of attending together.

In the spring of 2012, Jessica asked me if she could use our tickets.

"Sure thing," I said. "Who are you planning to take this year? Anyone special?" I teased.

"Oh, you know," she replied. "I'm taking a date. His name is Landon and he has a little brother, so I thought it would be fun to take him with his girlfriend." She always thought of others, so her plans didn't surprise me.

"Well, have fun and be safe," I said as I handed her the tickets.

"I will, Dad," she laughed. She kissed my cheek and headed out the door to finalize the arrangements with Landon.

About a month later, Jessica was over for dinner. We chatted amicably until I asked, "How is it going with your new young man?"

I saw Jessica stiffen slightly as she answered, "It's over, Dad." She offered nothing more but looked down and began to move the food around on her plate.

"What happened, Jessica?" I asked.

"He has a girlfriend," she quietly replied.

"A girlfriend," I said. "That was fast. How did you find out?"

She looked up at me and said, "I saw it on Facebook, Dad."

I felt so bad for her and such anger for this jerk I had never met. This Landon guy didn't deserve her. She was such a kind soul and beautiful inside and out. I knew I shouldn't say anything, but I couldn't help my anger. You better stay as far away from him as you can, sweetie. He sounds like a player," I said. All was quiet for a few moments, and I wondered for the millionth time whether I had given the wrong fatherly advice.

Then Maury spoke up. "If you're done with dinner, let's clear the table and have our dessert on the back patio."

Maury always knew how to smooth things over. And since she and Jessica were so close, I knew if there was anything more I needed to know, Maury would tell me later.

•••

Around the same time, we received Jessica's cell phone, Detective Kestner had found four men who had been involved in some way in Jessica's life over the prior five years. They each were questioned and released. But one man was moving from a "person of interest" to a "suspicious person" in *my* book. He was about a year older than our daughter and was the young man Jessica had taken to the rodeo. *Landon Baines.*

I kept up with Kestner weekly and he was

so good about giving me updates. While things moved slowly in the world of solving cases, I was strangely comforted by his willingness to keep me in the loop of information.

Early one morning, my phone rang as Maury and I finished breakfast.

I could see by the number it was Ray Kestner.

Over the weeks, we had begun developing a kinship and had dropped our surnames whenever we spoke with each other. And we did a *lot* of speaking.

I punched "talk" on my phone. "What's up, Ray?" I asked when I answered. I sat abruptly as I heard his words.

"I spent a lot of time questioning Landon Baines," he said. "He admitted being at Jessica's the evening before her death."

My head began to spin and I couldn't think clearly. I could see Maury looking at me with concern.

"What?" she mouthed. I just looked at her and tried to concentrate on Ray's words.

"He says he was with her but didn't know how she died. It wasn't a confession, but it is one more thread that placed him at the scene of the crime within the early morning hours when Jessica's died. And Steve, Landon smokes the same brand cigarettes you found in the garage."

"Can't you just arrest him?" I cried into the phone.

"No. We need every detail tied up tightly before we can do that. I asked him for a swab of DNA so I could rule him out as a suspect and he refused. He claimed his DNA would be all over her house since he had been living with her for about three months."

"That is a lie," I shouted.

Maury got up and came to me. She started rubbing her hand up and down my arm, and I found comfort in her calm presence. She leaned close to listen.

"Maury dropped by Jessica's all the time and had never seen evidence of anyone staying there, Ray. Right, Maury?"

She nodded in agreement.

"No cars, no clothing, no toiletries in the bathroom. That man is a liar and he is guilty."

Ray was silent a moment, then spoke. "Steve, I want you to listen carefully and understand what I'm saying here. I'm going to *keep in touch* with Landon. We aren't going to lose him. This man is no dummy. He is a bad dude and has a rap sheet as long as my arm. He is on parole for child abuse and has already violated his probation. I've questioned him several times and he is threatening to file harassment charges against me. I don't want anything to hang up this case, so I'm stepping into the shadows, so to speak, but keeping my eye on him. He will make a mistake and then we will nab him. So, you've got to stand back and be patient."

I hated hearing that. How arrogant of him to claim he lived with my daughter. She always had a heart for the underdog but she wasn't about dating them. As hard as it was, I paid attention to Ray and promised to wait some more. But before I hung up the phone, I prayed for Ray that God would not only give him wisdom in this case but that He would also protect him from Landon and his evil ways.

We continued on with our daily routine, trying to live as normal a life as possible under the circumstances. I tried to work, Maury continued building her strength back up and each night we knelt together and prayed for God to work in this terrible situation. The waiting was hard but we spent as much time as we could with our young grandchildren. Their innocence was refreshing to see in the midst of the dark road we were walking.

One morning, not long after that conversation, I was sitting in my leather chair reading God's word and Maury came in. She was quiet. She sat down across from me and waited until I looked up. I knew she wanted to talk.

"What?" I asked.

"I wasn't asleep. God gave me a vision early this morning. I'm telling you, I was awake," she said.

I put my Bible down and looked at her.

"I believe you," I said. "I learned long ago to pay attention to you when you say God has told you something. So, tell me what you saw."

"I saw my mom, and Jessica was with her. They looked happy and healthy. They were talking to one another and Jessica turned to me and said that Landon is the one who killed her. It was weird. She didn't look sad or distressed. She just looked like she was telling me a fact I should know. I can't explain it, but I absolutely believe that was God speaking through our daughter."

"Thank you, Jesus," was all I could say. What a comfort to be reminded that Jessica was safe and happy but I secretly wondered why God did not give me the vision. But that wasn't the way He spoke to me. I realized more and more that God spoke to whomever He chose and however He chose, and it was not really my business to question that. But I was a little envious that Maury got to see Jessica whole again.

Chapter 12
Dark Days

W E HAD BOUGHT JESSICA her house three years ago and we were in no hurry to sell it. It was strange comfort to know we still had a "physical" connection to our daughter. I visited often, just to look around. Eventually, we started cleaning out Jessica's personal affects and I began to sift through her personal papers. I wanted to see who she had talked to in her last months, where she spent her money and any other details I could find that could be helpful to the case.

One day as I was combing through her bank records, I came across a withdrawal I had forgotten about. In May 2012, Jessica withdrew $1,250 from her savings account. I remembered asking her what she planned to do with that money, and she'd told me she had loaned it to a friend who couldn't pay her rent, but would pay her back.

In July of the same year, Jessica had taken

$850 out of the bank and again I'd asked why. Because she'd been evasive, I'd dropped it. After all, she was an adult and was always careful with her money. Much later she admitted to her mother that Landon needed the money to fight for custody of his child. Turns out, it was a lie. We soon learned the money went for his bail when he was charged with child abuse.

Around the same time Jessica took the money out, I learned Landon was working for his brother as a manager of his vacuum cleaner store. He had Jessica answering the phone for free. I was annoyed, and had told her how I felt. "Besides," I told her, "you are going to school to be a nurse and need to focus on studying.

She listened and immediately quit working for him. I remembered feeling relieved to think we'd finally gotten rid of the guy.

But as I continued going through her bank statements, I saw that wasn't the case. In January 2013, Jessica again withdrew $850. I still didn't know where that money went, but I suspected it somehow went to Landon, the man she was with on the last night of her life.

It was now March, and Ray called to say Landon had suddenly flown to Hawaii for business. And he foolishly put it on Facebook, which Ray had been following. I was thrilled until Ray told me the bad news.

"Even though Baines is in violation of his probation by leaving the contiguous forty-eight states, Steve, no county in any state has the funds available to send men that distance to pick up a parole violator."

"So now what?" I asked.

I was getting very frustrated and so was Ray. To come so far and wait so long and then to have this kind of a roadblock. Ray said he was working on what the next step should be and assured me he wouldn't give up. I told him I wouldn't give up either and called on our friends to pray.

Not too long after that conversation with Ray, he called again. Excitement was in his voice. "Steve," he said. "You are not going to believe what happened."

"Did you get him?"

"Soon, Steve. Soon," he replied. "I called Mountain County's Judge Davis and had an interesting conversation with him. I let him know he had a parole jumper on his books. I told him he is our main suspect in a homicide case. He offered to cash in his airline miles to get two men to Hawaii to pick up Landon."

I let out a yelp and could barely contain my excitement. Maury was in the bedroom lying down, but got up and came when she heard me shouting.

"Hallelujah and praise Jesus!" I couldn't believe God had touched this judge's heart, someone who didn't even know us, and turned it toward our family.

I was reminded of Proverbs 21:1 which said: "The king's heart is in the hands of the Lord and He turns it whatever way He wishes." And God certainly did that for us. He turned the judge's heart toward us and our sorrow over our daughter. I hung up the phone, grabbed Maury, and danced her around the room.

"What on earth?" she asked.

I repeated my conversation with Ray and hugged her over and over. I couldn't stop smiling. God had certainly answered our prayers and we stopped to thank Him. That was the first night I actually slept.

It wasn't long until Landon Baines was back on the mainland. Once there, he was then interviewed by a beautiful young FBI agent. Being a ladies' man, he foolishly didn't request the presence of an attorney, which was his right, and he freely answered the questions the field agent asked. During the interview, he actually admitted to being with Jessica and stated she was alive when he was there. He also admitted he stole some of her belongings and that she wasn't breathing when he left. That was still not an admission of guilt where Jessica's death was concerned, but it was enough to incriminate him in her inability to call for help. If he was there, why didn't he call 911 or take her to the local hospital? And since he took her phone, computer, and car keys, she had no way to get help even if she had woken.

On June 25th, Maury's birthday, Landon was charged with violating his parole, which carried a mandatory sentence of fifteen months in jail. It wasn't the murder charge we were waiting for, but it did keep Landon incarcerated while more work was being done on the case. Ray told me since he was in custody, Landon *had* to give up his DNA. This was one more thread in the rope that was tightening around Landon's neck.

•••

In the summer of 2013, I was finally contacted and told Jessica's coroner's report was ready and that I could pick it up at the courthouse. I decided it was in everyone's best interest for me to go alone.

As I drove downtown, I cried the entire way. I felt such dread. Even though the funeral was months ago, I knew the report would make everything feel so final.

Once I got the document I went to my car, and decided not to wait until I got home to read it. Instead, I pulled it out of the manila envelope and just stared at it. It was so official looking, so devoid of feeling.

Taking a deep breath, I opened it and began to read.

"Decedent: Jessica Mary Branson."

Decedent? What the heck is a decedent? A quick check on my phone dictionary and I learned that a decedent means a deceased person. Why didn't they just say that? Better yet, they could have said *person* who died because that was what she was—a person. It felt so impersonal. Like if it didn't have Jessica's name typed at the top, it could have been any Jane Doe. Like my daughter was just another body to dissect and report on. But I continued to read.

The report gave Jessica's address, next of kin (that would be me), the date and time of the autopsy, and who attended.

There were people there, watching? I felt sick at the thought. But I knew I had to move forward. I had to know what it said before I showed it to Maury.

The report had given an assigned number to Jessica and then it described her age, height, weight, and physical description. It said she had blue eyes and waist length blonde hair. In my mind it should have said "big beautiful blue eyes" and "long, silky, honey-colored hair." *What is wrong with these people,* I thought. *They can't get anything right.*

I had waited so long and was eager to get the report. I thought it would validate that my daughter was innocent and someone was guilty. Instead, I was disappointed. It was just words that didn't represent who my daughter was, let alone who had taken her life.

But I pushed through my disappointment and

continued reading. The notes told what position the body was in when found, what she was wearing, and any markings on the body such as moles or tattoos. It then listed any medications found in her bloodstream. This was what I'd been waiting for.

Jessica had .10mg of Hydrocodone in her system. That certainly wasn't enough to harm her, but I wondered why she had taken it. Had she injured herself on her last ride? Had she been in pain and not said anything when we last talked? Had she taken the medication for "fun" like some kids did?

I wondered, but knew I would never have all the details of Jessica's life. There was a second drug listed in this section. Jessica had GHB in her system. The so-called "rape drug." My head began to spin. *What kind of low life would use a drug to have sex with a woman?* Just thinking about it made me ill.

Suddenly the report shifted into a more personal nature. I wasn't prepared for this. Each part of her body was described in great detail, and while I knew it was important to look for any body trauma, just reading the words of what was found felt so violating. I felt ashamed to be reading such intimate details. I loved my daughter, but I hadn't seen her naked since she was old enough to bathe herself, so it felt wrong to be reading these descriptions.

I skipped the rest of the report and moved to "cause of death." And there it was - the truth. Cause of death was listed as suffocation. This sick person, this animal, had drugged my daughter, probably raped her, and then killed her.

The next words on the paper felt like a punch to my gut: Manner of death: Homicide.

I began to tear up. I hadn't realized the emotional toll it would be to read the details of the report. *Somebody killed my baby girl.* I put the papers into the envelope and laid my head on the steering wheel and sobbed. I was a broken man. I felt crushed in spirit. But God promised His presence to the broken-hearted and saved those crushed in spirit (Psalm 34:18), and even in those moments of despair, I still felt His presence.

I drove home to Maury and showed her the report. Then, we faced our grief together. We thought the day of Jessica's death had rocked us to the core, but seeing the declaration of homicide on the paper showed us there are many levels of grief and as I read the report to Maury, something fractured inside us.

Chapter 13
Stolen Goods

JOHN 10:10 SAID: "SATAN comes to steal, kill and destroy, but Jesus said He came that we might have life and life abundantly."

It was October 1st 2013, one of Jessica's biological sister's birthdays. I was thinking about Jessica and how different her life would have been if we had not adopted her.

I tried not to entertain those crazy thoughts of "if only." You know the ones. They snuck into our brains whenever we experienced a traumatic event in our lives. "If only...I hadn't taken that job or bought that big house or gone to the store that day etc. etc." On and on it goes. Every scenario that would change the outcome of whatever tragedy had hit your life. The truth is, none of us are in control of our lives, but we are all under the illusion that we are, until we go through something that changes the trajectory of our course.

The Word of God said that He knew us when we were in our mother's womb. He decided our birth day and our death day. And He knew every minute of every day in between. He was so interested in us, that He had even numbered the hairs on our heads. Amazing. So, after I played the "if only" game in my mind for a while, I arrived at the thought that God knew *before* Jessica was born when He would call her home. It gave me some comfort to remember that *nothing* surprised God. He was there with her when she was born, and He was there with her when she left this earth.

The phone suddenly rang making me jump. I recognized the number.

"What's up, Ray?" I asked as a way of greeting.

"We found Jessica's laptop," he said.

"Really? Where was it?"

"Two states away, and you are not going to believe how we got it."

Now Ray really had my attention.

"Two young guys were in a Wal-Mart in this little town. They decided to do some shoplifting. But they got caught and ran out of the store. They jumped in their car and sped off. Stupid choice. Of course, Wal-Mart called the cops, and they pulled these guys over and searched their car. Those guys would have been better off staying in Wal-Mart instead of running like they did." He laughed.

"Wait," I said. "How do you know the laptop

belonged to Jessica and wasn't stolen from elsewhere?"

"We ran it through CODIS and the numbers matched. You know what CODIS is, don't you?" Not waiting for my answer, he continued. "It's a national data listing of criminal's DNA. And guess whose *number* was all over it? Landon's."

"Hallelujah!" I shouted into the phone.

"That's not all," Ray said. "Because they are in a different state, we can keep them locked up for a month while the paperwork is sorted out between the two states. And the best part is, these guys were so ready to give it up, they confessed immediately that they got the laptop from Landon, which links him to the robbery."

I could hardly believe my ears. God had miraculously given us another gift that only He could give. No one in a small town two states away was looking for Jessica's computer. But God knew right where it was and how to bring it home for evidence. I had been praying for God to bring justice for Jessica and it was clear He was answering in a big way.

•••

Time dragged by as we waited for Landon to be charged with our daughter's murder. Our court system moved so slowly. There was evidence to be found airtight, paperwork to be completed and filed, rights exercised.

The District Attorneys, or DAs, constantly changed, and during the time of the trial, we watched five come and go. Five. I'd felt so frustrated watching that, but I understand the logic. To ensure checks and balances, and ensure no DA favored any one lawyer or became biased for or against the plaintiff or the accused, they didn't allow them to stay too long on one case. I understood it, but it didn't make the waiting easier.

The one-year anniversary of Jessica's death was rapidly approaching and as we looked toward it, Maury and I began discussing what we should do on that date. Should we go away on a trip? Should we stay home and have family in? Should we visit Jessica's grave? What did one do to mark that first year?

I could hardly believe it had been a whole year. The days seemed long, but the weeks flew by. After much discussion, we decided to honor our daughter's life and to share that time with friends, family, and those who have helped us along the way.

December 15th, 2013, was a crisp, clear day. That evening we invited friends and family into our home for a memorial to Jessica's life. It was cold that night but it didn't deter anyone from joining us that evening. Even Detective Kestner had taken the time to join us. We had a house overflowing with many who loved Jessica and loved us enough to share our joy and our grief. It was comforting to know how many lives Jessica had touched in her short but vibrant life.

Christmas had always been a special time of year for our family, so our house was decorated for the holidays. The tables were laden with all kinds of goodies and the rooms were filled with people. Laughter and chatter was heard all over the house. After so much sorrow, it was refreshing to sink into life and absorb some of the energy present.

After some time of fellowshipping, we all put on our coats and trekked outside. As we stood in the cold night air, I looked into the black sky and silently thanked God for everyone who shared the memorial with us. I went to the front of the crowd and thanked them for their love and support during our harrowing and painful journey. Then, our granddaughter, Jaime, came up with a small group she had organized and sang for us. As they did, we each lit a small candle for Jessica. It was such a special time and somewhat healing for many of us.

The evening passed quickly and soon the voices lowered to a few quietly conversing while cleaning up the mess that always came with a crowd. I was sitting with Maury, who was pretty worn out from having to be up for so long when Ray approached me.

"Can I talk with you for a moment?" he asked quietly. By now, I had known Ray long enough to recognize when he talked in such measured tones, he had something important to say.

"Let's go into my office," I said and led the

way.

Once inside, I closed the door and offered him a chair. "This won't take long, he said. "I thought you would like to know that we finally have enough on Landon Baines to formally charge him with murder. His DNA matched the skin Jessica had under her fingernails. She also had GHB; the rape drug in her wine glass," he said.

Finally. I thought. We have waited so long.

He interrupted my thoughts and continued. "You know, if you hadn't helped in the investigation with extra information you gave and ideas you had about the case, it might never have been solved." *Thank you, Jesus! You have provided all we needed as you promised.*

He reached out and as we shook hands I gave him a quick hug. I thanked him for all the hours he put in to find Jessica's killer. Over twenty-five counties were involved, and over two hundred pages of documentation went into this case. That required multiple people putting in long hours for our daughter, who they didn't even know. I would *always* be grateful for the sacrifices made on Jessica's behalf.

As I watched Ray turn to depart, I called out, "You know it wasn't me who helped this case. It really was God."

Ray turned back and smiled, then he walked out of my office. I felt a smile on my face too because I knew Maury would feel as relieved as I did when she heard the news. It didn't bring our beloved daughter back, but it did feel like justice had been won.

•••

As I said before, Jessica had a kind and giving heart. She also loved beautiful things and since Christmas was a much loved occasion for us, I like to spoil my children a bit. The kids, of course, loved this and supplied me with long wish lists every year.

In November of the year Jessica died, we had received word that her birth mother had cancer and didn't have long to live. Jessica knew her biological mom and had kept up a relationship with her sisters. We all prayed for this dear woman, who had given us such a gift. But in God's sovereignty and mercy, He chose to take her home within two weeks of her diagnosis.

Jessica was worried about her half-sisters and told me she no longer wanted to get a lot of stuff for Christmas, but wanted Maury and I to use that money to buy gifts for that part of her family. We obliged her and it became a family tradition.

It was our privilege to reach out and share with them and their children. It always reminded me of how the Father above reached out to us and shared His Son so we could become part of His family. It's a tradition we keep to this day.

Chapter 14
Your Sins Will Find You Out

WHEN YOU WERE WAITING to go to trial, life crawled at a snail's pace. Each time we got close, the hearing would be delayed. Being patient was difficult. I kept in constant contact with our detective, Ray and I tried to encourage him by reminding him how many people were praying for him in his work.

I was always very aware of what a tough job he had. He saw grisly murder scenes, took in all the details he could, and then spent countless hours looking for the ones responsible for the crime. Then he had to take time out of his busy schedule to sit in court and be ready to testify before the judge. I couldn't imagine having that kind of job. Our situation gave me new respect for what it took to be a detective and not only look for a killer, but also deal with the grieving relatives.

Still, as we waited, God continued to tie things

together.

In April of 2014, a woman named Tiffany was caught trying to pawn some of Jessica's jewelry at a large jewelry store. Detective Kestner talked with the management of that store and asked for the information on who pawned the stolen merchandise. They were not very cooperative, but suddenly acquiesced when they were told they would be shut down for the illegal sale of stolen goods.

Ultimately, the jewelry store found out they had an employee who knowingly took in the stolen jewelry. That person was arrested and a warrant was put out for Tiffany. Somehow, she caught wind of it and immediately went on the run. But the police were relentless and stayed on her tail for an entire year.

Finally, after many months of living life under the radar, Tiffany turned herself in—nine months after pawning the jewelry and more than a year after Jessica's death.

She was eventually brought to trial and pled guilty to theft. She also admitted she had received the stolen merchandise from Landon and had pawned most of the stolen stuff a few days after Jessica's death. As heartbreaking as it was, it was just more evidence God was working behind the scenes.

I was still learning about being patient with God's timing, as the court dates were moved several more times. To this day, I didn't understand all the reasons why it took so long to get to court, but I did know God. So I spent my time running my business, caring for Maury and her illness, and writing thank-you notes to everyone I could think of who had helped us in any way.

During that time, my family and I also began to pray for the person who had killed our precious daughter. We prayed he would give his heart to Jesus and become a new creature, just like 2 Corinthians 5:17 promised. For as much as we had suffered by the actions of that man, and wanted justice, we did not want him to go into eternity without the Lord. We wanted him to stand before a judge and not stand before *The Judge of the universe*. So, we prayed. And along with praying for his soul, I began to pray for a spirit of forgiveness.

•••

God kept working on me throughout the year, but near the end of November, my faith was really put to the test. It was the evening of November 22nd 2014, a date I would never forget. I was getting ready for bed when I came out of the bathroom and heard what sounded like a loud pop.

I yelled, "Maury, are you okay?" She didn't answer.

I rounded the corner just in time to see her lying on the bed with her eyes rolled back in her head. I dropped down beside her and could see what looked like a drop of blood at the corner of her mouth. She wasn't breathing.

Crying out to the Great Physician, I said, "Please God, we have come so far, tell me what to do."

At first, I thought maybe she had choked, so I got behind her and did the Heimlich maneuver. Nothing happened.

"Please help me, Lord," I continued to cry. "You gave her life and now she's not breathing. Please give her life back."

Pulling her to the floor, I started CPR. How could this be happening? I had already lost so much. Would I lose Maury too?

Realizing she was biting her tongue, I tried to pry her jaw loose at the same time I was calling 911. Suddenly, she began breathing erratically.

"Hurry!" I commanded the person on the phone. "She is barely breathing."

EMS finally arrived after about fifteen minutes. By then she had started to breathe slowly but at a more normal rhythm. After the EMT checked her vital signs, they put her on a stretcher and carried her to the ambulance.

I could see she was beginning to come around and didn't want her to be worried.

"I'm with you Maury," I said. "Don't worry. It's going to be okay."

I ran to my car and backed it out of the garage so I could follow the ambulance to the hospital. As I drove, I prayed, "Lord, I have no power over life or death. Only *You* know the numbers of our days. Please be with Maury. Please Lord, bring her back to me. Thank you, Father, for helping me, and please give me strength for what is coming next."

I continued the twenty-minute trek behind the ambulance and then broke off when they pulled up to Memorial City Hospital. Heading to the closest parking lot, I parked, jumped out of the car, and ran to the emergency room door, all before they pulled Maury out of the vehicle.

Although my body felt tense, my spirit held peace. I knew God was totally in control of this situation and once I had settled into that truth, I was calm.

Maury was admitted to the hospital for three days. During that time, I went between work and the hospital. When I couldn't be there, Joy stayed with her mom. The doctors did a battery of tests and decided her fall was due to a seizure. Finally, after putting her on anti-seizure medication, they discharged Maury from the hospital.

The only thing we could do at that point was thank the Lord for rescuing us in our time of need and continue with our wait. I knew God was sovereign, but I couldn't have imagined losing Maury as well. We'd always been so close, but the time since Jessica's death had bound us even more closely. Our hearts were irrevocably linked, and I was so thankful she'd been spared from death.

Chapter 15
Heading To Court

IN JANUARY 2016, WE were told that the trial was finally scheduled for mid-February, over two years after Jessica's death. So, Joy and I went to talk to the newly appointed DA in preparation for the trial.

We walked into the conference room "A" and shook hands with a tall, handsome man. He looked young to me but I assumed he knew what he was doing. We sat down in the offered chairs. I began asking a few questions.

The young man was flanked on both sides by women, which I found odd. But who was I to question how he did his job? Each time I asked a question, however, he would defer to one of the women beside him. He didn't answer one question. Actually, he never really spoke to either one of us at all, once we sat down. It was a strange and frustrating experience.

Joy and I had been praying about this meeting for so long and now we were feeling unsettled about the whole thing. When we were finally free from the meeting, Joy and I walked out together.

"What are you thinking?" I asked.

"I don't know, Dad," she replied. "That was weird. Either the new DA hasn't spent any time reading about our case and doesn't know the details, or he is so new, he doesn't have any power." *That doesn't make any sense. Isn't he the one who answers to the ultimate authority?* I began to feel unsettled about the whole thing.

"Well, I don't want to go to court with *him* on the case," I grumbled.

We went home perplexed and discouraged. It wasn't long before I figured out one of the women was actually the Assistant DA and the other was *her* assistant. The young man had just gotten hired and was "shadowing" the women to see how things were run! I was not happy that no one made it clear who were dealing with. We soon got word the trial date had been moved again. Only this time, we were glad.

The new court date was to be April 14th, which meant more waiting. And more working. And more asking God for patience and endurance as we tried to live a normal life in the midst of an abnormal situation. I had learned a very important life lesson though. Work had driven me for so many years. Had consumed me at times. But losing a child, almost losing a wife, grieving daily, dealing with the slow and daunting criminal prosecution process, my priorities had shifted. God first. Family second. Work was a requirement of living, but it no longer held my heart and main focus. God was kind indeed.

One week before the trial, I received a call from the young DA. "Mr. Branson," he said. "This is Maverick Jones. You need to come down here and talk to us."

I scoffed at the thought. His words sounded so condescending. Why would I need to inconvenience myself for this guy? But I didn't say it.

"We were just there a few weeks ago. What do you want to talk about?" I asked.

His reply surprised me. "We have made a decision."

He was being really evasive, which put me on edge.

"A decision about what?" I asked.

"Please just come downtown and meet with us," he said.

"All right," I replied. "We'll be there soon."

I sighed as I punched the "end" button on the phone. I immediately called Joy and told her what the DA had said.

"Is there any way you can get off work to come with me?" I asked.

"Of course, Dad. I'll tell my boss and then

come to the house and get you." She was so blessed to have a boss who understood the stress and strain we'd been under and had graciously told her anytime she needed off, just let her know and she would make it happen. I was so grateful for her generous nature.

Next, I went looking for Maury and found her resting on the sofa with a questioning look on her face. She must have heard me talking.

"What?" she asked.

"Oh, it's probably nothing. That kid DA, Maverick, wants me to come down and talk to him about some decision he has made."

"Okay," she said wearily. "I'll get my shoes on." She started to sit up but she was still a very ill woman and had little stamina left.

"Lie down, sweetheart," I said. "I've already called Joy and she is on her way."

Maury complied and sighed with relief. "I'm sorry I'm of no help to you. I can't do all the things like I used to."

"Don't worry about that," I assured her. "I am fine. You just rest and Joy and I will take care of whatever Maverick wants and we'll be back soon. And if you are a good girl, I'll bring home a pepperoni pizza. You've always loved pepperoni." I kissed her on the forehead and started toward the bedroom to get ready. I heard a giggle and as I turned, I saw a sweet smile cross her face.

Within thirty minutes I heard Joy's traditional greeting at the door.

"Knock, knock," she said as she came in. "Hi, Mom." Her voice was cheery as always as she walked over to give Maury a kiss of her own.

"Hi, dear," was Maury's response. Her eyes were still closed so I knew she was fatigued. "Take good care of your father. I've been promised a pepperoni pizza and he better deliver."

"I will," Joy promised and turned to me. "Let's hit the road, Dad. We don't want Mom to be wondering where her pizza is." And out to her car we went.

"I'll drive, Dad," she said. "You lean back and rest your eyes for a bit. I know the way." Always sensitive of others' needs. I took her up on her offer. I leaned back and closed my eyes as Joy drove toward the court house.

Once there, as we pulled into the parking lot, I began feeling uneasy so I turned to Joy and said, "Let's pray before we go in." We bowed our heads, and I prayed for God to go before us and to strengthen us for whatever lay ahead. We got out of the car and headed in to see Maverick.

When we reached his office, I was not surprised to see female colleagues in attendance. Other than to greet Joy and myself, he did not speak. He let the ladies do the talking.

We sat down and got to the business at hand.

One of them looked me straight in the eye and said, "Mr. Branson, we have already made a plea bargain."

"What?" Joy and I said in unison.

"What kind of bargain?" I asked.

The woman continued. "Mr. Baines will plead guilty to murdering your daughter and will receive a sentence based on manslaughter vs. capital murder.

What? I thought. We have come so far to be given so little? Lord, I asked for justice. Is this what You want?

I sat there dumbfounded for a few minutes. Then I spoke up. "So, what does that mean in terms of Landon's punishment?"

She spoke again. "Mr. Baines will receive six years in prison for manslaughter and two years for the theft of Jessica's possessions."

My mind was reeling. I couldn't believe my ears. *We had waited four long years for that? Six years for my dear daughter's life?* It didn't make sense to me and I was having a hard time comprehending the plea bargain.

I think I was in shock because I stood up, shook hands with each person there, thanked them for the information and walked out. Joy almost had to run to catch up with me. I wasn't sure where I was going, but I knew I had to get out of that building before I fell apart.

We reached the car and as I yanked the passenger side door open, I realized Joy was already crying. That brought me back to reality. I reached over and held her as best I could. *My little girl, Joy*, I thought. *I can't forget I have TWO daughters, not just one.*

"It's okay, honey," I crooned. "I'll be fine. Just give me a minute."

I held her while she cried and I calmed down. Soon her tears turned to sniffles. I let go of Joy and reached into my pocket for Kleenex.

"Here, dry your face, sweetheart, and let's go home. Do you think you can drive or do you need me to?" I asked like any sane father would do.

"No, I can do it," Joy said as she dried her tears and cleaned her face.

We talked all the way home about God's continued care for us, and we both came to the conclusion that even though we would still go to court for the "official" sentencing, maybe it was better that Maury not have to sit through the long hours of a trial. I knew she wasn't in any condition to sit on a hard, wooden court bench due to her continued back pain. She was still physically and emotionally fragile.

I could settle with things as they were when I thought about what was best for Maury. Even if part of me still wanted more. So I continued to pray for justice for Jessica.

Chapter 16
The Sentencing

APRIL 14TH 2016 WAS the day Landon Baines was to be sentenced. Joy and I went together to watch the proceedings. Maury was at home in bed, unable to join us since she had just been released from the hospital again, after another serious physical issue had shown up. I hated to leave her at home without me, but I *knew* I was meant to be in that courtroom. I had the right to read a Victim Impact Statement, so I had one prepared, and prayed I would be able to get through it. It helped me knowing Maury was at home lifting us all up before God's holy throne of grace.

Joy and I arrived an hour before the appointed time. That was a good thing because to get to the elevators that led to the courtroom floors, everyone had to pass through a metal detector. And that took a lot of time.

When we finally arrived at Courtroom 6, we

saw lots of people already seated. Looking around to find an empty pew, we were surprised but comforted by seeing Jessica's loved ones. Both of her half-sisters, her best friend, Heather, Heather's mom, and a cousin who had a close relationship with our daughter were all there. We slid into the wooden pew beside this little band of supporters. There were hugs, a few tears and soft words being spoken among us. Finally, we settled in to wait.

I noticed there were around twenty people on the docket list, attorneys, a court reporter, the bailiff, and the judge. That made the count about fifty people who would be viewing our private pain. I didn't expect so many strangers to be there as spectators, and while I didn't appreciate what felt like insensitivity toward us, I knew it wasn't a personal insult. And I trusted that God wanted these people to be in the room when I read my statement.

Suddenly, a door on my right opened and in walked Landon and his lawyer. Landon was in an orange jumpsuit and handcuffs. He was seated near the front, with his back to us. That's when Heather's mom and Jessica's cousin began to weep. Heather had spent a lot of time with Maury since Jessica's death. She had felt so guilty knowing Jessica had continued to give in to Landon's demands even when she too had warned her away from him. She, like us, couldn't work out what Landon's motive was for murdering Jessica. The crime never made sense.

The intensity in the room was palpable, all eyes had turned toward us, and I knew others could sense the seriousness of the moment. It's also when I realized all eyes had turned toward us. But God was there with us.

Joy told me later she happened to glance up at a woman who was staring at us. The woman looked into her eyes and quietly said something. Joy strained to hear. "Jesus, hold this family. Jesus, hold this family," the woman kept repeating. Such spoken words were never sweeter to the ears, than those of the stranger who prayed them for us.

Meanwhile, I was listening to the woman next to me, who was praying in Spanish. I knew a little of the language so I was aware she was praying for us too. How wonderful that God placed His people where He wanted at the perfect time they were needed. To know that those women, strangers to us, but not to God, were lifting us up to the throne of grace was incredible.

The experience changed the way I prayed. Now, when I see someone who looks like they had a hard day or were down on their luck, I immediately begin praying for them. No questions, no judgment. Just passing on the gift someone else gave to us that day in court.

All eyes moved to the front of the room as the judge invited Landon to stand before the bench for sentencing. We all sat still and listened intently as he made sure Landon understood the charges brought before him and what was taking place.

"Yes," was all Landon said.

The judge then said to Landon, "Do you understand that if you accept the plea bargain then you give up the right to an appeal?"

Again, Landon simply responded with, "Yes."

The judge then read each of the charges against Landon and the sentence for each. He proclaimed the charge of felony for theft and pronounced the sentence of two years in the state prison. He then read the plea bargain for manslaughter and pronounced a six-year sentence, also to be served in a state prison. The judge then asked, "How do you plead?" and we heard Landon say the word we already knew.

"Guilty."

There wasn't even time to process what had transpired before the judge called me up to the front to read my Victim Impact Statement. I stood only a few feet away from the man who'd killed my daughter with such mixed emotions rolling through me, and yet my body felt numb. I had asked God to go with me and speak through me, and I counted on Him doing just that.

I placed an eight-by-ten picture of Jessica beside me for all to see, and then I read the words on the page before me.

"We are gathered here today for the memory of our loving daughter, sister and friend, Jessica Mary

Branson. We miss her and love her dearly. We want to express our view as a Christian family. We thank God for the twenty-six years of life that Jessica had been given. Jessica was a wonderful young woman who loved everyone and wanted to help everyone she met." I then went on to read a few of the stories about her standing up to bullies for others, her speaking before the Senate at such a young age, and more importantly, her accepting Jesus into her heart when she was eight years old. I told the court of her plans to be a nurse and how much she loved her horse and her two dogs. I concluded my time of speaking with, "But this story is not about Jessica. It's about Jesus. We believe Matthew 25:31-46, when it says the final judgment will be brought by God and not by man. We have also forgiven Landon for the murder of our beautiful daughter, Jessica, because that is what Jesus would do."

Landon looked up at me and quietly said, "Thank you."

"That is what Jesus said when they crucified Him on the cross. 'Forgive them, Father, because they know not what they do.'" As I spoke those words, a man sitting behind Joy loudly said them with me. "Forgive them, Father, because they know not what they do."

When I was done, I thanked the judge for the opportunity to speak for our family, picked up Jessica's picture, and made my way back to the pew where our little group sat. Many were watching us, some were crying, but all felt the weight of our experience.

The District Attorneys took us outside the courtroom to explain some last-minute details about parole and getting registered on the TexasVine.org. Texas Vine is an organization that contacts the victim whenever a convicted offender comes up for parole. The victim then has the right to attend the meeting or send a letter giving his or her input to the parole board before a decision is made.

As we were standing there in the hallway discussing these details, one of Landon's defense attorneys walked up and said in a very monotone voice, "Mr. Branson, I am very sorry for your loss. I would like to ask your permission for Landon to write you a letter." *He can write it but I'm not sure I can read it.* But I responded with, "Of course."

Ms. "Monotone" continued. "He really wanted me to give you a note today, but I told him I would prefer to ask your permission first. And I want you to know," she continued, "while Landon was in jail, he became a Christian and has trusted his life to Christ. He has been attending group meetings."

She also said Landon was very sorry and each time he spoke of Jessica, he said what a good person she was.

I knew God could do big things, but never once did it cross my mind how much He was moving, not just in our lives, but in Landon's as well. It was mind-boggling, and yet one of the most confirming things I'd ever heard.

I handed the attorney a Bible and asked her to give it to Landon when he was sent to prison. She promised me she would give it to him and said she believed he would treasure it.

I could hardly believe the conversation I had just had. I looked at Joy, she looked at me, and we both started praising God for what He had done through Jessica's death.

As we continued to walk toward the door, a man across the hall saw us and shouted to Joy, "Can I give you a hug?"

Joy immediately responded with, "Yes," so he ran over to us to give that hug.

He excitedly told us, "I was in that courtroom. I heard what was said."

Joy responded with, "It was all because Jesus is alive. He gave us the power to impart to Landon what's been done for us."

The man was nodding profusely as he exclaimed, "I know, I know. You lived out the way Jesus Christ would have responded to that man if He was here today."

He *was* there that day. We all knew it—everyone, believer and non-believer, saw and felt the power of God in that courtroom. I knew it in the depth of my soul.

Joy and I moved out the door, somewhat

stunned, but also humbled, grateful and joyful. I couldn't fully explain the feelings of relief we experienced. But I knew this: we had gone in as victims and come out victorious in Christ.

Was I happy that Landon was only incarcerated for eight years for his crimes? No. But I did trust that God put him in the right place to hear his need for Jesus and his heart responded. For *that*, I could be at peace.

•••

Joy later shared with me an experience she had when we were standing in the hallway, listening to Landon's attorney. She told me the Holy Spirit spoke these words into her heart: "Joy, do you truly believe and desire what you prayed for?"

She said she remembered the times she had prayed for Landon's salvation and the many conversations we'd about forgiving Landon and praying for his redemption.

And then Joy heard in her spirit, "Because, I go after men's souls."

Joy said she felt like God was saying to her, "Don't miss it. Don't miss the point of what I have accomplished."

As she told me the story, she said, "You know, Dad, Jesus is about His purposes and not ours. We wanted justice. But He is about saving the souls of men for eternity by the forgiveness of sins through His death on the cross."

She was absolutely right.

•••

By April 21st 2016, I was preparing to celebrate another birthday when the phone rang. I answered and was surprised to hear Ms. Monotone on the line.

"Mr. Branson," she said.

"Yes," I answered tentatively.

"This is Ms. Blont, the Defense Attorney for Landon Baines."

"Yes," I said again. It had been six months since the trial. *Why was she calling me now?*

"Mr. Branson," she continued. "Landon has written that letter for you and I would like to send it if you are still agreeable to his request."

Such dry words for such an emotion-packed request.

"Yes, I am happy to receive his letter."

She offered to have it delivered to me and I accepted. The courier arrived about an hour later. I took it into my study and sat down. After a moment sighing, I shot up a prayer of, "Lord, be with me," and opened the envelope.

It wasn't a long letter, but in it Landon again thanked me for forgiving him. He felt so ashamed about his actions, was thankful he met Christ, and was reading his Bible. He was currently studying to become a minister. Landon also said something very significant. He said he couldn't believe that God would work such a miracle for *him*.

And wasn't that true for all of us? God worked miracles in our hearts that changed us forever. 2 Corinthians said: "If any man be in Christ he is a new creature. The old things are gone and the new has come." Because of His sacrifice on the cross, He made a way for that change to happen. And *none* of us deserved it.

•••

I didn't know why God allowed Jessica to be taken so suddenly and so early in life. There were times I struggled with grief about what was and what wouldn't be. But I did know we would see Jessica again, because Maury, Joy, Rick, and I had all come to the realization that we stood just as guilty before God as Landon had. And we each have bowed our hearts before the Lord and asked Him to come into our hearts, cleanse them, and rule within us forever.

Where do you stand? Are you guilty of something? Of course you are. Every one of us is guilty of *something*. And everyone needs the Savior. Including you.

Chapter 17
The Mysterious Works of God

MANY PEOPLE HAVE ASKED me how I dealt with the hatred I could naturally have for the killer of my daughter. I wish I had a good answer for that. This has been a hard road for sure, but God has used it to do a good work in me.

Early on in the darkest part of our journey of grief, I ran across a story about a preacher whose daughter was murdered at thirty-two years old. That got my attention.

Someone had asked this dear man why he didn't seem to hate the man who took his daughter's life. He stated he knew he didn't have time in this life to waste it on being angry. That really spoke to me. Life is short, and even though I have grieved intensely and still have some days filled with sorrow, I have learned to give those feelings to the Lord.

I can even feel some empathy for this man who

committed this terrible crime. I have no idea how he grew up, what he had endured in his own life and how he got to a point where he could take a life.

Everyone starts out as an innocent little baby. But something went terribly wrong in Landon's life to bring him to the place he was when he met Jessica. And because of it, he has to carry the burden of his actions for the rest of his life.

But even through the horror, our God still reigns. Just as Joy had expressed, God will go to any length to save one man's soul. While it is still a terrible thing that Jessica's life was cut so short, her death indeed speaks loudly to God's hunger for captured souls.

Satan is the great deceiver and certainly deceived Jessica into believing Landon was a nice man who just had a hard life. Just as the Bible says, Satan prowls around like a roaring lion, seeking someone to devour (1 Peter 5:8 NASB). On the outside, it looks like Satan did exactly that. It seems like he was able to destroy Jessica, her family, and Landon and his family. That's quite a feather in the cap of the father of lies.

But look closer. God brought such beauty out of ashes.

There *will* be suffering in this world, but "The eyes of the Lord roam throughout the earth to strengthen those whose hearts are fully committed to Him." (2 Chronicles 16:9). If you are suffering right now, remember He desires to strengthen you as He has strengthened us.

Jessica is now with Him, enjoying the beauty and peace of eternity in Heaven. Beloved family members were there to greet her when she arrived. And now they wait for the rest of their loved ones to show up.

What a great reunion that will be.

Epilogue

STEVE AND MAURY CONTINUE to love the Lord, walk together as a couple, and enjoy their child and grandchildren. I asked them recently what is different in their lives since Jessica's death. Their answer? Steve told me that this experience has made them bolder about proclaiming the goodness of God and the miraculous ways He worked through Jessica's death. He said, "Nothing is as important as serving the Lord. Besides, it all belongs to Him. We are just caretakers while we live on Earth."

Joy and Rick have moved to a deeper walk with the Lord and when you are near them, you can feel incredible peace emanating from them. They laugh and live with grateful spirits as they watch their children grow. And they rest in the knowledge that someday they will see their loved ones again when God calls them home to be with Him.

Landon-On March 3, 2014 Landon bowed his

heart before the Lord Jesus Christ and accepted Him as his savior. He is still growing as a believer and is spending his time reading God's Word and ministering to other inmates in prison. He is teaching and preaching to all who will hear. His letter to Steve is full of praise to God for all He has done in his life and for the freedom he has felt having accepted salvation through Jesus. He also told Steve that the grace and mercy shown him in their declaration of forgiveness during court was the most profound experience he has ever had. And isn't that true for all of us? Once we experience true forgiveness from someone, it wipes away our guilt and gives us a fresh start. How much more exhilarating to receive forgiveness from God for ALL that we have done. And that kind of forgiveness is what He offers. We pray God increase His flock through Landon's dedication to spreading the hope of the gospel in a place where hope is not usually found.

And the author of this book? She has been forever changed by having the privilege of walking through this experience with the family as the events unfolded and seeing up close God's miraculous provisions for all involved. It is my prayer that as this book goes forth, God will use it to comfort and encourage others and to reveal Himself to many souls.

So, what about you? Have you come to see that life is short, no one is guaranteed tomorrow, and none of us are exempt from tragedy? If your heart tugs at this, that is the Holy Spirit prompting you to get down on your knees, confess to God that you are a sinful person (as we all are), and ask His son, Jesus, into your heart and life. Then find a good church that teaches the bible where you can meet fellow believers who will encourage you and pray for you as you embrace that new life.

And most of all: get a hold of a Bible. The Bible is truly **B**asic **I**nstructions **B**efore **L**eaving **E**arth. There are many new translations now that are easy to read. Find Matthew, chapter one and start reading. Your eyes will be opened to all kinds of things. And you will never be the same.

Remember, God will do anything to capture those He loves. He is all about chasing men's souls. That includes yours.

To God Be The Glory!

Acknowledgements

Even though God called me to write this book, there are so many people who took part in making it come to fruition and without them you would not be reading Jessica's story.

I must first thank the *real* Steve who openly shared his personal and sometimes painful information so that the details of this book would be accurate. And in the midst of writing, when I would be feeling unsure about my abilities, a text would show up with encouragement from him. Thank you, Steve for being such a cheerleader during the long months of working through the process. I count it a privilege to call you a brother in Christ.

To my husband Mike, who shared in many hardships over the last year, I thank you for being my anchor during the storms that would surely have taken me down had it not been for your steadfast ways. I'm so blessed to be on this journey with you.

To my daughter M.E. Carter, who guided me through every step of the process to get to the finish line. Her knowledge and generous spirit encouraged me to learn how to do "big girl" writing. Thank you, M.E. for being patient with every interruption I caused when my computer would not cooperate! I love you and am so proud of the way you are going for your dream. May it come true beyond measure.

To M.E.'s book club who prayed for me during many dark days of pain while working on this book. I may not have met you in person but I'm honored to have you as sisters in Christ who cared enough to lift me up when I couldn't even stand.

To Marion, who not only went over the manuscript with a fine-toothed comb but who shared her expertise and gave suggestions to make this book be the very best it could be. I learned so much from her. Thank you, Marion for your thorough work and for your encouragement. Your kind spirit really speaks to my heart.

To Alyssa, who did a great job formatting and captured the very essence of this story on the beautiful cover. I am blown away by your talent!

And finally, to the most important one-my heavenly Father who called me to write and poured His words through my fingers. I am honored to be your servant.

MJ Michaels

49289028R00093

Made in the USA
Columbia, SC
20 January 2019